Spirit Wings

Dedication

In every single person's life there are spiritual mentors and giants who go before us and make us who we are. They help mold us and give us example, inspiration and insight as they too have fought life's giants on their knees. Recently, I have reconnected to some of my spiritual mamas and women/men whose authenticity and authority in the Spirit inspired me to keep going through the hard. They were the wind beneath my spirit wings as I wrote this book. Marzelle Newman, Patty Stansell, Wetona Duffee, Charlotte Spears, Lana Staudenmeir, Joyce Sepulvado, Ann Tew, Ruth Howard, Connie Holman, Vergie Walker, Jeanine Mosery, and so many more I could not list all. Just know that the time on your knees and living through the storms is seen and shared.

Spirit Wings
Reflections of God Moments Book 13
copyright © 2025

All Scripture quotations are taken from The Message, copyright © 1993, 2002, 2018 by Eugene H. Peterson. Used by permission of NavPress. All rights reserved. Represented by Tyndale House Publishers.

Scripture taken from the New King James Version®. Copyright © 1982 by Thomas Nelson. Used by permission. All rights reserved.

Written by: Donesa Walker
Design by: Will Baten
Edited by: Kelley Inderman

*The payoff for meekness and Fear-of-God
is plenty and honor and a satisfying life. Proverbs 22:4*

What does God see when He sticks His head out of Heaven and looks at you?

Are we ready to be fueled up with His power and might? Are we anticipating and waiting in breathless excitement for His power or are we pretending we have fuel while we hobble from station to station?

Does He look at us and see a string of zeros, empty, useless pretenders or are we striving to be the God ready, God expectant people He desires to fuel with His power?

Key thought for today:

Running on Empty?

Yesterday, I had to stop for gas because my car was running on empty and I know it will stop when it runs completely out. Today, I had to stop for spiritual gas because I was running on empty and I know what happens when I run completely out. As I was reading, I noticed that Psalms 14:1-4 and Psalms 53:1-4 are exactly the same. But while the 5-7 verses are similar, it is important to note the difference. In verse 5 of both texts, verse 5 starts the same but in chapter 14, the psalmist notes that God is in the generation of the righteous while in chapter 53, it says they were in great fear where no fear was because God has scattered the bones of those who come against us. Verse 6 goes back to being the same. When we run on empty, it matters what we fill our lives back up with in terms of fuel. My boys are big on healthy protein and bodybuilding so they fuel for the purpose of increasing their ability to remain strong and healthy because they want their bodies to build and grow. I often fail to fuel my body properly and well, most of you know all my health stuff. I like how the version of the Bible called The Message puts this: God sticks His head out of Heaven and He looks around for someone who is God ready and God Expectant. He is looking for that one of us ready to be fueled and filled, empowered with the top line of God fuel. Gabe, my youngest, is a pilot and he worked for a while on the flight line while he was in training fueling planes and jets. It matters what kind of fuel is put into an engine. I mean it does if you want real power or pseudo power and it matters that the right fuel is used or the engine doesn't work. I tell parents every day at my office about fueling the brain and hydration because it matters. It matters also that you do not run on empty because empty causes breakdown of the engine whether it be car, plane, body, brain or spirit. Fuel matters and filling up at the right time with the right fuel matters. Pretenders. That is all God sees. He looks out from the psalmist point of view and sees nothing but pretenders. People running on empty trying to prime the pump of the church and shepherd others but they are empty. If you pull up to a pump to get fuel and there is none, you go to another, then another, then another until you get whatever it is you need. If you jump from church to church hoping to get fuel, you miss the point. The church isn't the fueling station. God is. The church is simply the gathering place of those who are willing to gather and set the fuel to flame. The church is the place where we should be seeing the flow of the fuel spreading like flames in a wildfire. But following a person or cause in a particular manner doesn't fuel you. It should challenge you. It should ignite you, spark you, motivate you but the fueling station is in His word. What does God see when He sticks His head out of Heaven and looks at you? Are we ready to be fueled up with His power and might? Are we anticipating and waiting in breathless excitement for His power or are we pretending we have fuel while we hobble from station to station? God is looking for one man who is God expectant or one woman who is God ready for fueling so He can pour out His power upon us. Does He look at us and see a string of zeros, empty, useless pretenders or are we striving to be the God ready, God expectant people He desires to fuel with His power? If we are running on empty emotionally, spiritually and it is affecting you physically, He recommends that we get to His filling station promptly and begin to seek His presence. He is eager to fill us with His presence and His anointing so we can be used by Him. Quit fueling up on the talking heads of politicians and pretenders. Go to the source of all power. Align with Him and allow Him to fuel you with what you need to move His purpose forward in your life.

As it is written: "Look! I'm putting a stumbling block in Zion, " "which is a rock that offends people. " "And the one who has faith in him will not be put to shame." - Romans 9:33

That rock in your path that is blocking you from receiving the promise is Jesus. What will you do about Him?

Why did God put Jesus as a rock in our path?

Key thought for today:

Stumbling Stone?

"Jacob have I loved, Esau I have hated". Wow! That scripture always caused me misunderstanding in my life as I puzzled how God who created all-especially these wonderful twins of destiny could choose to love one and despise the other. It is counterintuitive to all that is God. God is love. How can He hate a child and cause issues for this one throughout his life? He didn't. God wasn't talking about the physical twin but the spirit. I have two boys-not twins. They are both dearly loved and were dedicated to God at birth. They have strong opinions and their own lives now but sometimes one or the other will feel like or state that one is loved over the other by me. Certainly it isn't true. It isn't in me to love one more than another. I simply love them. I will do whatever I can for them. God's love isn't limited to one person or group or race either. God destined the walk with man and gave choice. The choice created the chaos but yet God loved enough to send His own son to solve the great divide created by the sin choice. Romans 9 is a hard chapter to absorb because it has a lot of things in it that seem counterintuitive to who God is. I chose to feature verse 33 for this reason. God said He placed a stone in Jerusalem that makes people stumble. This stone is Jesus. He is the rock that makes people fall because if we will trust in Him and bow to His will and ways, we will never be disgraced. We get so caught up in our own will and desires that we fail to seek His will and ways for us. This is what He was saying in the Jacob/Esau quote. Jacob was a conniver/liar who was full of tricks. He was dearly loved and pampered more by his mother because she knew the promise that God had told her was that Jacob would be greater. Esau followed the law. Esau did everything right as he was asked and yet, the stumbling block was in his path. He didn't value what He had as his birthright. He felt it was his so he despised it as just a thing that was. He sold it to his brother for a bowl of soup because he didn't see anything but the law. He didn't see God. He only followed the rules. He didn't experience God. The Esau spirit is the "just let me be and do it my way" spirit. It is an independent and self reliant spirit that God hates. He put Jesus on the line to redeem us from that same spirit. Adam/Eve made the choice of self over God and it cost them and us. Cain made that choice and it cost him and his whole line as well as the life of his own brother. We can go from the beginning of scripture to today to see that the choice is bow by choice or stumble into a fall. Every knee will bow eventually but those that choose now to follow God and sacrifice self and selfish desires, will receive promise and eternal life. The clay (us) doesn't decide what we are to be or do. The potter (God) forms us, makes us and provides our purpose. It is in the yielding that the clay becomes what the potter desires. If the yielding isn't complete, a flaw forms and must be broken and reformed until the yielding is complete. I believe Esau made his peace with God as he forgave Jacob once he understood. I believe God's purpose was and is worked despite us many times because we are stubborn. That rock in your path that is blocking you from receiving the promise is Jesus. What will you do about Him? Trust Him and give Him all, then the promises are yours until the end of time. Parents can give all they can to make their children happy but ultimately happiness is a choice. My sons have the same choice I did and you do. What will you do about Jesus? He is the stumbling stone that makes our plans go awry. He is the rock in our path blocking us from our dreams. He is. That seems harsh. God put Jesus there for a reason. He is the choice of the great divide. He is the bridge to God. He is the rock of choice. He is the promise. He is God's son and God's purpose. Jacob warred with God and came out a victor because of his yielding not because of his own ability. He was tenacious about knowing who God is. Every example in scripture had struggles but they had the choice too. We want Him to be the God of promise and He is but first, we must cross the Great Divide by the choice. First, we stumble, then we choose. What will You do about Jesus? It is your choice.

The payoff for meekness and Fear-of-God
is plenty and honor and a satisfying life. - Proverbs 22:4

What is Plenty?

Enough?

Satisfying?

Riches?

Glory?

Fame?

Power?

What does it take to reach this place of contentment despite your circumstances?

Key thought for today:

Plenty Satisfying?

What is Plenty? Enough? Satisfying? Riches? Glory? Fame? Power? I looked at many versions of this verse including the original Hebrew for context and meaning. Chapter 32 of Proverbs is a collection of wisdoms or a plethora of great sayings. Most of them deal with wealth, riches, money, etc. History tells us that Solomon wrote these Proverbs down to instruct his children when he was around 50, after he had been king for around 20 years. He had learned a thing or two about life and he wanted to put it down for inspiration and instruction to others. It is written in a poetic way with lots of the wisdom which was the gift of God. No matter what interpretation I view, this man of infinite wealth and wisdom composes a verse of satisfaction, provision and honor being gained through the genuine respectful fear and humbleness before God. Solomon understands that his life is not his own but belongs to God. This man of means in power, authority and riches shares the secret to a satisfying life. Worldly culture lies to us by stimulating an insatiable desire for more, more, more. Have it your way, get more, possessions and wealth and power and political gain but all of this is lies. The wisest man who ever lived other than Jesus-given wisdom by God Himself-gave us the key to a plenty, satisfying and rich life. He told us the honor, riches and a fullness of life come as wages or as pay for humble respect for Who God is. Enough, plenty satisfying, replete, full, arrived, satiated, and contentment are all words describing this feeling. Right now, in this very moment as I sit before God, in His presence with my home filled with my children, I am plenty satisfied. I am content and confident in Him. I am at rest in Him. I am blessed. I can count the things that can be better or I can be plenty satisfied in Him and I choose fullness of Joy. I choose the payoff. I choose to sit and soak in His presence. It is enough. It is plenty satisfying for all I need, want, and desire. What does it take to reach this place of contentment despite your circumstances? Respect that God is who he says He is and humbly ask Him to be enough. That's all. God, I need enough, I need you. I need your presence and your provision, I need your calm and peace and contentment to surround me. I surrender my, I wants into you're enough. I trade my desires for your riches. I long for you alone. That is the life of plenty.

Be brave. Be strong. Don't give up. Expect God to get here soon. - Psalms 31:24

David won the battle against the Philistines and Goliath by a small stone and God's mighty hand. Why did Saul not see that he is God's anointed? Why is David having to run for his life?

Stand up! The battle is upon you. Be brave! Trust His word. Expect Him to show up and don't give up! Be brave, strong and expect God! What does it mean?

Key thought for today:

Be Brave?

When I look at these lights, I picture the throne of God and the reflections of the sea of glass coming down on us. In Psalms, David is in a tough place in chapter 31. He has been chased and harassed by Saul along with his armies for no reason other than worshipping God, doing what he was told to do and being well liked. Saul has an ego problem and decides his kingdom is at risk so he decides to go after David. The truth is that David is God's anointed now and he knows it but in the midst of these years of struggle, it all seems mighty unfair. He won the battle against the Philistines and Goliath by a small stone and God's mighty hand. Why did Saul not see this? Why is David having to run for his life? David is confused and frustrated as he starts talking to God in this song but as he continues, he comes to the place of realization in verse 23: "Love God, all you saints; God takes care of all who stay close to him, But He pays back in full those arrogant enough to go it alone." Psalms 31:23 MSG. Then he takes that message of realization to others in verse 24 which is our focus today. Be brave. Expect God. Don't give up! Expect God to get here! Be strong! Expect God to get here Soon! God does take care of all of us who stay close to him. He will fight your battles that He has already won. Quit running and believing that you have to hide in caves. Stand up! The battle is upon you. Be brave! Trust His word. Expect Him to show up and don't give up! Be brave, strong and expect God! What does it mean? God is a God of expectations beyond your wildest dreams. I am not talking about a name it, claim it type of mentality but rather a know it, state it. Know His promise, walk in it. State it. Encourage yourself in it. Believe it. I watch many Christians walk around beat down with their burdens never realizing who God is. I myself get discouraged and down sometimes with the burdens of life because I try to go it alone. This is what David was doing as he was running and hiding in caves for years. He kept trying to go it alone and then he would touch God for a bit and refresh. Then he would get spooked and try going it alone again....constant cycle. Because he is like us, human and walking around in a world of fear under people who are running things from a place of perceived power. God is the only one who is all powerful! We need to quit running and gear up for battle. Armor up! Face up! Stand up! We need to get the rocks out of our shoes and put them in our slingshots of anointing then fire away at the giants in our lives. We need to remember that we are anointed kings in the kingdom of the Almighty. We are victorious not victims! We are overcomers because He overcame! We are a powerhouse of mystery and might because we are indued with His Spirit. Not by our might, not by our power but by His Spirit we will overcome!

"It's urgent that you listen carefully to this: Anyone here who believes what I am saying right now and aligns himself with the Father, who has in fact put me in charge, has at this very moment the real, lasting life and is no longer condemned to be an outsider. This person has taken a giant step from the world of the dead to the world of the living. -
John 5:24

Will you reach out to Him in your frustrations, close your eyes and take a giant leap of trust into His waiting arms of love?

Why is this so urgent?

Key thought for today:

Giant Step?

The abyss was wide and I was extremely uncertain that it could be crossed or resolved. Then I heard His voice, "close your eyes, take my hand and take a giant step." I trusted him so I reached out and grabbed his hand and without a moment's thought leaped into his arms. I will never forget that moment. I was on my honeymoon in Chattanooga, TN. The magic of that trust is still there because in the dark places of life, I can still grab his hand and step into his arms but when the storms batter us together, we do the same for our God. We reach out to Him in our frustrations, close our eyes and take a giant leap of trust into His waiting love. He is always enough! In John, he calls it a "giant step from the world of the dead to the world of the living." Anyone who believes what I am saying right now and chooses to align with God can at this very moment take that giant step of trust into a real, lasting life that is no longer condemned by death. Anyone. God loves each and every one of us and He desires that all take this step. It is urgent. Each day could be the very day that Christ returns and the urgency is here more and more as the signs of the times spread like wildfire. I see people prepping for a time of lean times and people wondering why toilet paper has shot up to ridiculously high prices. Medicines are hard to find and it is getting harder and harder to find the foods and things you are used to having. Warnings of banking collapses and money changing on dates in the near future to all digital currencies, earthquakes, hurricanes, famines, diseases....all signs...Jesus is preparing to return. The earth senses it and labors as a mother preparing for birth. The whole of nature is aware that the King of Kings is coming soon. It is time to take that giant step. Come into the warmth of His love. Simply reach out by saying, Jesus, here I am taking your hand and giving you all of me as I take a giant leap into your arms. Then trust Him. It is worth it.

If we claim that we experience a shared life with him and continue to stumble around in the dark, we're obviously lying through our teeth—we're not living what we claim. But if we walk in the light, God himself being the light, we also experience a shared life with one another, as the sacrificed blood of Jesus, God's Son, purges all our sin.-
1 John 1: 6-7

What if you could move the hand of God on your own behalf, on behalf of others or on behalf of the nation? Why can't you?

What are you doing about the IFs? Are you allowing them to block promises because you are not doing what needs to be done or are you walking in His truths?

Key thought for today:

What IF?

On Sunday, this was my pastor's question and sermon. God wants a response from you to Him if He is going to move in your life. My pastor, Ray Holman, made some truthful comments and points that God has continued to work into my being the last two days.

What if you could move the hand of God on your own behalf, on behalf of others or on behalf of the nation? We can with the right choices. It is unfortunate that our Christian culture today is about waiting on God to do something for us instead of us doing something for Him. We can move the hand of God. We move the hand of God by His word and our choices. We can move the hand if we take our responsibility to God seriously.
The conditions of promise come from acting on the IF. Our responses to God, His words and His commands, affect our relationship and determine our future.

It isn't about if God is going to move, it is about you moving. Are you going to do the IF, so He can move on your behalf? If occurs in scripture 1,521 times and every time it is a choice on our side. It calls for your attention because this word is most often an indication that something significant is coming up. So when you come across this word, concentrate more and focus on what follows the text you are reading.

The first IF is the key to opening every other promise of blessing in our life.

1 John 1:6-10 MSG
"If we claim that we experience a shared life with him and continue to stumble around in the dark, we're obviously lying through our teeth—we're not living what we claim.
But if we walk in the light, God himself being the light, we also experience a shared life with one another, as the sacrificed blood of Jesus, God's Son, purges all our sin.
If we claim that we're free of sin, we're only fooling ourselves. A claim like that is errant nonsense.

On the other hand, if we admit our sins—simply come clean about them—he won't let us down; he'll be true to himself. He'll forgive our sins and purge us of all wrongdoing.
If we claim that we've never sinned, we out-and-out contradict God—make a liar out of him. A claim like that only shows off our ignorance of God."

"But what does it say? "The word is near you; it is in your mouth and in your heart," that is, the message concerning faith that we proclaim: If you declare with your mouth, "Jesus is Lord," and believe in your heart that God raised him from the dead, you will be saved. For it is with your heart that you believe and are justified, and it is with your mouth that you profess your faith and are saved."
Romans 10:8-10 NIV

What are you doing about the IFs? Are you allowing them to block promises because you are not doing what needs to be done or are you walking in His truths?

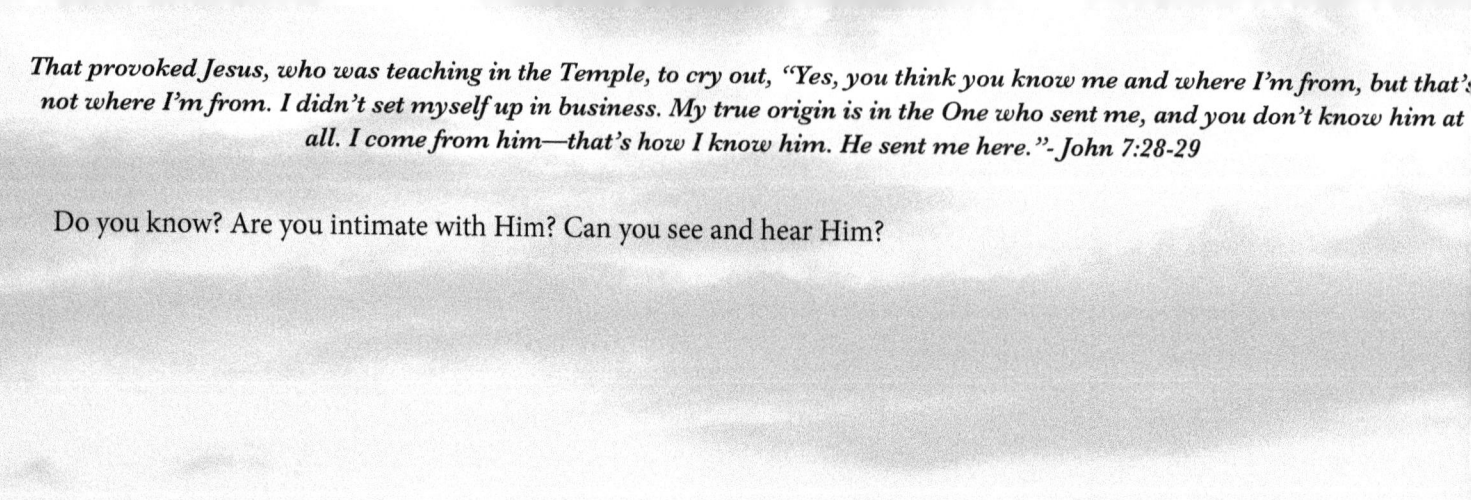

That provoked Jesus, who was teaching in the Temple, to cry out, "Yes, you think you know me and where I'm from, but that's not where I'm from. I didn't set myself up in business. My true origin is in the One who sent me, and you don't know him at all. I come from him—that's how I know him. He sent me here."- John 7:28-29

Do you know? Are you intimate with Him? Can you see and hear Him?

How do we become more intimate with Him?

Key thought for today:

Do You Know?

There is an intimacy in being "in the know" with someone. I think of levels of intimacy and see FB friend, acquaintance, business or client relationship, friendship, etc. as all being important but they are all at a disadvantage or distance as they are not "in the know". Being intimate with another means knowing or understanding more. In this 7th chapter of John, Jesus is teaching in the Temple but the people are mouthing and mumbling because they cannot accept His authority and skill at teaching because they think they know Him. They know His family, lineage and birth which was looked down upon as lowly, poor, uneducated and lessor. They do not know Him as from the tribe of Levi who were the Priests and teachers. He is The High Priest greater than any religious authority ever, yet they do not acknowledge Him for who He is because they could not see the true Him-they were not intimate in the knowing. Intimacy in friendship comes from openness and sharing with another. There are times in my life where I have tried very hard to befriend someone but they were closed off to me. They had a certain way with them that was superficial or guarded. These are people who chose not to become more intimate with me because they closed off the connection. My husband is like this with others as he is very guarded while I am extremely open. The truth is that the level of knowing comes not from years of being acquainted but rather intimacy of relationship. I have friends from years ago that I haven't seen in many years but they truly know me and see me so we are closer than people I see daily. The question to ask is: Do you know me or just know about me? Intimacy is the knowingness of relationships. Jesus said to them, you think you know me and where I'm from but that's not me nor where I'm from. My true origin is In the One who sent Me, and you don't know Him at all. Wow! The religious leaders, the people who claim to study and have knowledge are put into a place of the uninformed. They are not "in the know". Do you know? Are you intimate with Him? Can you see and hear Him? His Spirit speaks to us and through us and for us if we dwell in "the knowing". When I was young, I would read scripture like Genesis 4:1, "Adam knew Eve, his wife and then she bore a son, Cain." without an understanding of what "knew" meant. Scripture uses the term knew/know as a level of intimacy. The word Know is used over fifteen hundred times in scripture! God's word is in the know-it is the know because it is of God. His word is the way to intimacy with Him. Dive in. No degree required. Begin to know Him like never before. Get "in the know" with God by learning and leaning into Him! Do you Know Him?

On the final and climactic day of the Feast, Jesus took his stand. He cried out, "If anyone thirsts, let him come to me and drink. Rivers of living water will brim and spill out of the depths of anyone who believes in me this way, just as the Scripture says." (He said this in regard to the Spirit, whom those who believed in him were about to receive. The Spirit had not yet been given because Jesus had not yet been glorified.) - John 7:37-39

How do we prime our pump?

How do we create a discipline and desire for more of Him?

Key thought for today:

Are You Thirsty?

Would it surprise you to know that thirst is worse when you have a little but not enough? When you are thirsty and you have a taste, the thirst ramps up because the body/brain signals that there is a source. In this seventh chapter of John, as Jesus had been teaching, many became more thirsty to learn more. A little education leads to a desire for more like a little information primes a pump. A little of God makes you hungry for more of Him so that you seek Him. A spiritual habit of super hydration will create a thirst for more of Him and in return bring more of Him to you. It is in creating the desire that we must focus. This requires discipline to go to the source and whet the appetite for more of Him daily. I often have to remind my parents that they need to hydrate more because as we age, our body systems are not as efficient and we hold less. Drinking more means eliminating more so often as we age, we drink less and this causes dehydration, brain fog, joint issues and more. Priming the pump by sipping means that our body begins craving more fluid, more source, and more filling. Then we begin to feel better in our bodies and brains. The same is true for our spirit. When we prime our spirit daily with habitual time in prayer and reading of scripture, our souls begin to seek more of Him, the true source. Our hunger and thirst grow and then the Rivers of Living Water begin to flow to us and through us to others. The priming is the discipline which is the key to more. You cannot grow dividends without investing. The more you invest, the more you grow. This is the principle of faith. Invest and reap. If you never risk the priming, you will never experience the waterfall of blessings that are in Him. Taste and see that He is good. When it feels that all around you is failing, trust in Him to be The Source. Thirst is only quenched by drinking and if you have never tasted, you will never know that His Living Water is like nothing else. Challenge yourself to prime the pump and begin to super hydrate in His love by reading His word and spending time with Him.

But you, God, shield me on all sides; You ground my feet, you lift my head high;
With all my might I shout up to God, His answers thunder from the holy mountain. - Psalms 3:3-4

Tidewater-Psalms 42:6-11 Where are you walking?

Are you in the tide pool of His love or are you diving deep into His presence?

Current of change-Isaiah 43:1-4 Are you willing to change?

Mindset of Praise-Psalms 3:3-6 Will you choose His peace?

Faithboard-Ezekiel 3:12-13 Will you choose Faith?

Key thought for today:

Faith Surfing?

Tidewater-Psalms 42:6-11

"When my soul is in the dumps, I rehearse everything I know of you...Chaos calls to chaos, to the tune of whitewater rapids. You're breaking surf, your thundering breakers crash and crush me. Then God promises to love me all day, sing songs all through the night! My life is God's prayer....Fix my eyes on God— soon I'll be praising again. He puts a smile on my face. He's my God."

Where are we walking? Are we in the tide pool of His love or are we diving deep into His presence? When we walk along the edge we only experience the splash of goodness instead of the depths of His love. It is our choice.

Current of change-Isaiah 43:1-4

"But now, God's Message, the God who made you in the first place...."Don't be afraid, I've redeemed you. I've called your name. You're mine. When you're in over your head, I'll be there with you. When you're in rough waters, you will not go down. When you're between a rock and a hard place, it won't be a dead end— Because I am God, your personal God, The Holy of Israel, your Savior. I paid a huge price for you: That's how much you mean to me! That's how much I love you! I'd sell off the whole world to get you back, trade the creation just for you."

The current is the place that changes us. It can be a riptide or it can be a waterfall. It can be a place of cleansing or a place of refreshing but it is a place of change. Not all change is fun nor desired but change is necessary to growth. Embracing change can be a way to open our eyes to new possibilities and sometimes we get set in our ways so God has to bring a tidal wave or a tsunami/hurricane to shake us up to what He wants to do through us.

Mindset of Praise-Psalms 3:3-6

"But you, God, shield me on all sides; You ground my feet, you lift my head high; With all my might I shout up to God, His answers thunder from the holy mountain. I stretch myself out. I sleep. Then I'm up again—rested, tall and steady, Fearless before the enemy mobs Coming at me from all sides." Mindset is a choice. We choose to praise through good and bad or we choose to go to dark places. Our mindset matters. The brain feeds on our mindset. Change your brain, change your life. We know this as brain trainers and yet so often we dive deep into the muck of complaining and whining about our situations. When we are in the deepest of storms in our lives, this is when our mindset matters most. Peace isn't the absence of storms in our lives but rather the confidence in Him through the storms. I love the song "Praise You In This Storm" because that is where the mindset shifts into the place of confidence in who He is rather than what I am. It is the place where I realize who I am in Him.

Faithboard-Ezekiel 3:12-13

"Then the Spirit picked me up. Behind me I heard a great commotion—"Blessed be the Glory of God in his Sanctuary!"—the wings of the living creatures beating against each other, the whirling wheels, the rumble of a great earthquake." Getting up from being beat down by the storms is not easy. I have always admired surfers. Truthfully, I am not as brave as it would seem. I like to skydive but I am fearful of drowning so I stay away from deep waters. I don't waterski or surf because I can be out of control and I do not like that feeling but the truth is that often that is exactly where God takes us. He takes us there because it is only in the places that we cannot control that we will rise up on the Faith Board because we have no other choice. I can take care of myself until I cannot. I am independent until I am not. I am strong until I am weak. I am confident until I am wiped out. The place of fear is the place of faith. The place of loss is the place of gain. The place of doubt is the place of faith. When you get to the place that He is all you have, then you will rise above all else. When the waves come at you, instead of running for shore, run deep into the waters of His love, trusting the Peacespeaker.

"You're blessed when you get your inside world—your mind and heart—put right. Then you can see God in the outside world. - Matthew 5:8

Today we each have a choice: inside or outside, which will you allow to dictate your life?

Key thought for today:

Inside or Outside?

A storm was on its way as I could feel the pressure on my body and could see it on the radar. Alerts were flashing on my screen that high winds with large hail were headed my way but all I could think was that my baby was leaving home today. He's grown. He's graduated college but he is still my baby. Both of my boys set off on journeys today in their outside world. Life changes and I can see God's hand in it so much. Just like I saw His paintbrush in the skyline last evening, I know He paints my mind with Calvary's brush of love daily. There is an old song that I love called "Lord, Paint My Mind with Calvary's Blood". It tells of how the pages of our mind hold memories and how sometimes these memories are not what we want them to be. Some things in life are not as we desire by time, effort or circumstance but in each one, if we choose, we can see God in them. It is our choice. In the book of Matthew, Jesus says we are blessed when we get our mind and heart-the inside world-aligned with God because then we see Him in the outside world. Clouds come to cover the sun; storms shake our world in tough situations but our outside world doesn't dictate our inside world. We have a choice and we know who holds tomorrow. All we must do is align our inside world securely in Him and He will direct the outside. I do not like storms. They make me a nervous wreck. I cannot control them. I can control me. I can choose to put my trust in the One who is always there and sticks closer than a brother. No matter what your storm or circumstance that is battering your outside world, take a deep breath, whisper His name then lean into His capable arms. When you focus on Him being on the inside rather than the storms that are on the outside, all will be made right. The storm has passed; my sons have gotten on their journeys and my inside world is all right. The quiet is only broken now by the birds chirping as they celebrate a wonderful time of fresh water, a bath and renewal. The plants are celebrating an influx of living water and I am basking in the presence of the Son. Today we each have a choice: inside or outside, which will we allow to dictate our lives? I choose the Peace Speaker who controls the winds and waves. I choose the Sky artist who paints the sunrise and sunset in brilliance. I choose Him who knows me better than I know myself. I choose to allow the inside world of blessing to become my outside view.

"You're blessed when you can show people how to cooperate instead of compete or fight. That's when you discover who you really are, and your place in God's family. - Matthew 5:9

What is our place in God's family?

Who are you?

Key thought for today:

Who are you?

As we go about our day-to-day, it's easy to question who we are. It is easy to see ourselves changing as we go through significant changes in our lives from career changes, marriage, having children to all the aspects of being a parent, then to empty nesting and on and on. It is very easy to lose ourselves, and to forget who we are. God called us for a specific purpose and we are His. He calls us the sheep of His pasture, and He tells us when we can show people how to cooperate instead of compete, that is when we truly discover our place in God's family. Our place? What is our place in God's family? Our place is as his sons and daughters. Our place is to reign with Christ as subject to Him. Our place is not the place of authority, but the place of humility. Our place is finding that we are not competitors, but we are there to uplift and to lead others to Him through our lives. It is not our job to see who can be the best. It is not our job to see who can be the top dog. It is our job to show the way to Him who loved us enough to send his own Son, the only way to Heaven. I am fascinated by the beatitudes and how they show us, as Jesus spoke so simply to the people on that hillside, that we are blessed by putting Him first and ourselves after. Who are you? The "who" you are is the truth of who He is in you. If you are in Him, then you are His and that is who you are.

"You're blessed when your commitment to God provokes persecution. The persecution drives you even deeper into God's kingdom.. - Matthew 5:10

What is driving you deeper in God's kingdom?

Key thought for today:

Blessed or Blended?

Recently an acquaintance gave me a backhanded compliment. They uninvited me to an event because they decided to have a stripper and knew I would not approve. She was right. I do not think that taking advantage of another person's body for the purposes of lust is aligned with God. I often have people not invite me to certain things because they choose to indulge in alcohol or other things I do not participate in. I am not judging them, they have seen a difference in me and know what I believe. I live loud and love loud. I have not missed out on one thing in life because I have never touched a drop of alcohol. I have not missed out because I stand for what I believe in. Truly I do not interpret this type of ignorance as persecution but some do. A friend and I had this conversation this past week. She told me how she was trying to recover from alcoholism but struggling because every Chamber of Commerce event she attends serves alcohol. I told her I just don't attend those that make it about drinking. If serving alcohol is more important than my business, then so be it. It is bad for your brain, your body and your spirit. I truly believe that is why they called them "spirits" because you are drinking of fleshly fulfillment. More crime has been committed due to alcohol than any other weapon from drunk driving to murder. Alcohol dulls the mind and causes poor choices due to lowered inhibitions. Now, that is not the direction I intended to write at all. Persecution is whatever drives you deeper into God's kingdom. Persecution can be harassment or harsh words or bullying but it also can just be a pressured choice to join karaoke at the bar or spend the time with God instead. It could come in many forms. The blessing comes from the commitment not the persecution. The blessings come because you choose to not be carried away by the tide of human emotion or peer pressure but rather to choose time away. It can be fasting in prayer rather than social-izing at lunch. It can be voicing an unpopular opinion on social media because it is a truth you stand for on God's word. Persecuted people don't always realize they are persecuted. They often stand out so much in God's favor and blessing that the persecution doesn't faze them. What is driving you deeper in God's kingdom?

All you saints! Sing your hearts out to God! Thank him to his face!
He gets angry once in a while, but across a lifetime there is only love.
The nights of crying your eyes out give way to days of laughter. - Psalms 30:5

Emotions run high as the days are long and the pressure is great. The diagnosis may be grim or the stressors of life seemingly unbearable but the choice is there: cry or laugh? What will your choice be?

Key thought for today:

Crying or Laughter?

Emotions run high as the days are long and the pressure is great. The diagnosis may be grim or the stressors of life seemingly unbearable but the choice is there: cry or laugh? Tears of sorrow can become peals of laughter in a moment. As I sat working with a precious sweet girl at my center, I saw her emotions swinging wide and hard. The challenge of reading seemed too much but oh so desired. She struggled and fought until the burden brought tears then a hilariously funny phrase turned the sorrow into tears: How now brown cow! I have no idea why it was so funny, but perhaps it was the funny voice I used or just the relief of the pent up stress...but whatever it was, peals of laughter erupted and delighted her into joyful giggles. Reading, the challenge from moments earlier had just become fun for the first time! Once in a while, God has had enough of our nonsense but He always comes back to love. The nights of frustration result in days of laughter as we celebrate in song and thank Him for all that He has done. The choice to sing and laugh in the confidence of love dispels the emotions of negativity and weeping. It inspires us to feel His love and joy. We all struggle through seemingly impossible circumstances or waiting places that seem to have no end but we will have laughter over crying when we choose to sing our thanks to Him despite the situation. Choose joy. Choose light! Choose love! Choose thankfulness. It is a choice. Emotions exist. Emotional stress can overwhelm us and set us back but if we choose confidence in His love then we can find delight and laughter through the hard stuff just like a child choosing to find hilarious joy in a nonsensical phrase. She found reading and I found laughter! She found release from the moment of stress and I found her smile which was contagious. Our confidence in His love is like contagious laughter in the midst of trying circumstances. No matter what you are going through, choose Joy!

But you, God, shield me on all sides; You ground my feet, you lift my head high; With all my might I shout up to God, His answers thunder from the holy mountain. I stretch myself out. I sleep. Then I'm up again—rested, tall and steady, Fearless before the enemy mobs Coming at me from all sides. - Psalms 3:3-6

What if we truly began to believe that with faith ALL things are possible? What if we decided to be fearless rather than brave?

Are you ready to step out into fearlessness rather than bravely walking through your day?

Key thought for today:

Fearless or Brave?

Fearless means without fear while brave means moving forward despite the fear. These words are used synonymously but it matters when you are reading to study that you understand the meaning of the words thoroughly especially in God's word. The Psalmist says God shields us on all sides so we are grounded in Him, our heads are lifted high and we can shout with all our might as He answers thunderously from His holy mountain. Then the psalmist says, we can stretch out in sleep before Him, confident in Him so that we awake rested, tall in Him and steady, Without fear before an enemy mob. David wrote this as he was on the run for his life. He found his confidence in God and it removed fear. I often hear how brave David was against the lion and the bear and Goliath. This is true that he was a brave young man who stepped out against things that make grown men quake but it isn't true that he stepped out because he was brave. He stepped out in confidence because there was no fear when God shielded him from that attack of the enemy. Yes, that is right. Fear is an emotion of attack that the enemy uses to silence us and limit us to what we can be and where we can go. The devil wants us to lack in God confidence because then the insidious emotion of fear keeps us from walking tall against the giants in our lives. We begin to look at mortal swords and shields instead of the God shield while we walk in confidence with our rock of His word in the slingshot of His power and might. Just imagine what could happen if every one of us that say we believe, truly began to walk in God confidence with no fear towards the future, the circumstances nor our surroundings. What if we truly began to believe that with faith ALL things are possible? What if we decided to be fearless rather than brave? God confident rather than God secure? Mountains would move. Cities and countries would change. Souls would be clamoring to come to our churches and into our lives. What if? Are you ready to step out into fearlessness rather than bravely walking through your day? I am. God, help me begin to walk in God confirming confidence instead of the bravery of …. God can, but I am not sure He will. Help me begin to walk in assurance and full recognition of who You are in my life! Let me be a vessel of your love to all I see and a truth seeker, God confident, fearless warrior for you!

When the Feast of Pentecost came, they were all together in one place. Without warning there was a sound like a strong wind, gale force—no one could tell where it came from. It filled the whole building. Then, like a wildfire, the Holy Spirit spread through their ranks, and they started speaking in a number of different languages as the Spirit prompted them
- Acts 2:1-4

What is it that you are believing for and feeling His call to you to do? Isn't it time you gathered together with others in His Spirit to experience who He Is?

Key thought for today:

All Together?

As I sit here in Washington DC, I am amazed that so many people from different nationalities and backgrounds are here and we struggle to agree on anything. I watched today in sadness our nation's capital in disarray, disrepair and disagreement. The hand of God moves without us but if we are to move the hand of God then we have to be "in one place" in our hearts and minds. I know we are so filled with our own desires, thoughts, wishes and such that we miss what happens when we yield to the place of Him in our lives. In Acts, it says they were all together in one place and without warning there was a sound of a strong wind that no one knew or expected and it filled the room. The SPIRIT of God arrived and filled the room so that every person began speaking in others tongues or languages. They spoke real languages and testified to God's goodness without them knowing the language they were saying but they knew in their heart that they were together in awe and worshiped together, Him. I walked in these awe inspiring buildings and places in my country's capital city and saw the awe, heard the awe spoken in languages I didn't know. Languages and words I didn't understand flowed but I understood the sentiment. The power of God doesn't rest in one person or one place, but it is like a fall of water made up of drops of living water that have such a powerful force together that they are an awe-inspiring force. Together. To gather. Two separate concepts yet when intertwined with The Holy Spirit, it is a supernatural force that has unfathomable power and strength. When our Congress agrees on legislation, it can be a powerful force as it can change direction for our country. When we agree as brothers and sisters in Christ, it can be even more powerful for at that moment we invoke the authority of God Himself and that is when His Spirit and His wind of change can impact the whole Earth like a wildfire driven by a ferocious wind. Gathered together to gather His will invoking change by His Spirit doesn't require physical presence but it does require agreement. What is it that you are believing for and feeling His call to you to do? Isn't it time you gathered together with others in His Spirit to experience who He Is?

What is the best advice you could ever get?

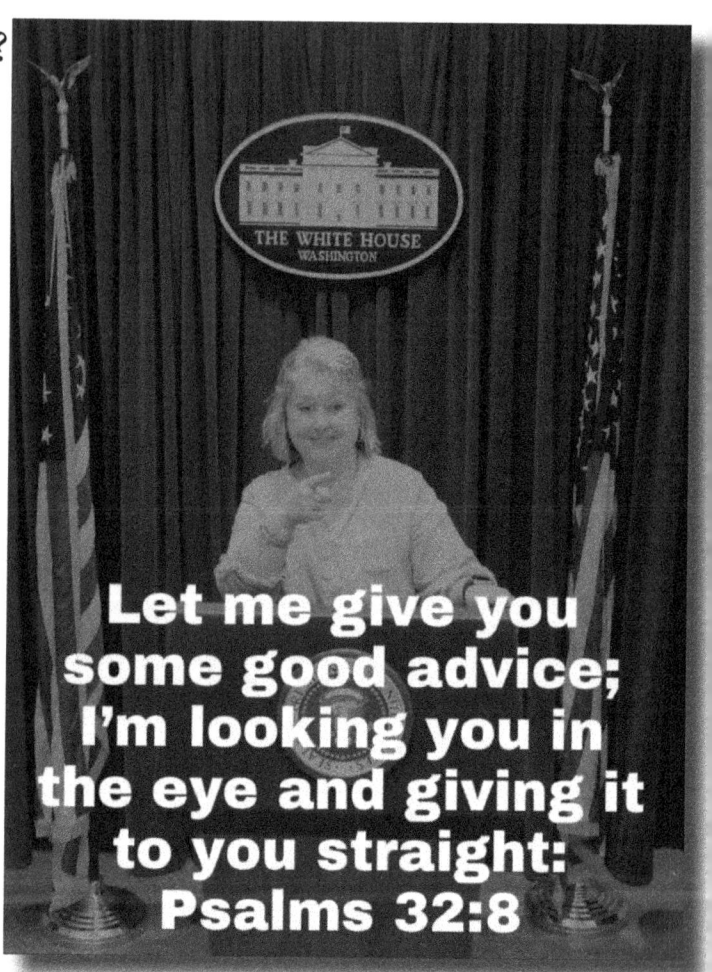

Key thought for today:

Good Advice?

In fun and truth, this picture has a lot of both. The White house is the place I grew up but not The White House in Washington DC. My dad is a preacher and a pastor. Those roles are the same yet vastly different just like the White house and The White House. My maiden name is White and the house I lived in most of my formative years was actually white also but it was vastly different from The White House although my dad was President, Dictator and Leader....He was also very much subject to who God is. Understanding who you are starts with understanding who He is. God is God and there is no difference in who He is whether the house you inhabit is white in paint color, white in race, white in name or White as in authority in government. We are all called to the same authority. In Psalms, David advised, ""Don't be ornery like a horse or mule that needs bit and bridle to stay on track." God-defiers are always in trouble; God-affirmers find themselves loved every time they turn around. Celebrate God. Sing together—everyone! All you honest hearts, raise the roof!" Psalms 32:9-11 MSG version or "I will instruct you and teach you in the way you should go; I will guide you with My eye. Do not be like the horse or like the mule, Which have no understanding, Which must be harnessed with a bit and bridle, Else they will not come near you. Many sorrows shall be to the wicked; But he who trusts in the Lord, mercy shall surround him. Be glad in the Lord and rejoice, you righteous; And shout for joy, all you upright in heart!" Psalms 32:8-11 NKJV

The Word is the same. We who acknowledge and celebrate God in His place for who He is will be instructed, guided and taught in His ways and mercy will surround us as we trust in Him, but if we are stubborn in our refusal to acknowledge the ways of the Lord and slow to follow Him, our lives will be filled with sorrow. God isn't subject to government, race, creed, deed or our opinions. He doesn't need our advice nor does He fall under our rules or authority. All authority is His. Once we learn to lean into who He is and not who we want Him to be or who we think He should be, we begin to acknowledge His authority and authenticity. At that moment, we find His love on every side surrounding us. We find His forgiveness, His mercy, His faithfulness, His provision and His will. Shout for Joy, be glad, sing, and rejoice because He has all authority. Let me give you some good advice: Acknowledge Who He is. Celebrate Him. Worship Him. That is the answer to whatever you are needing. It is the only answer you need.

Jesus said, "'Love the Lord your God with all your passion and prayer and intelligence.' This is the most important, the first on any list. But there is a second to set alongside it: 'Love others as well as you love yourself.' These two commands are pegs; everything in God's Law and the Prophets hangs from them." - Matthew 22:37-40

Passion means fervently, unabashedly and unapologetically in favor of something to the point that the emotion is rarely self-controlled. What if we truly loved God like that? What if we loved Him so much that it didn't matter to us what we looked like to others while in worship to Him? What if we loved Him so openly that everyone who knew us, knew we were completely and totally passionate about Him? What if our intellectual pursuits followed our passionate love for Him?

Who is in your path today? Are you looking to share His love with passion in prayer and wisdom?

Key thought for today:

Passion, Prayer and Intelligence?

"Love the Lord Your God with All Your Heart, Soul, Mind and Strength and your neighbor as yourself" are the words I have heard repeatedly all my life. These are foundations of who I am in life because this was how I was trained. I cannot help but thoroughly embrace this version told through The Message though because it speaks to me on a different yet powerful level. Passion, and Intellect are often thought to be in competition or angst with prayer yet here the three are intertwined together. Passion means fervently, unabashedly and unapologetically in favor of something to the point that the emotion is rarely self-controlled. What if we truly loved God like that? What if we loved Him so much that it didn't matter to us what we looked like to others while in worship to Him? What if we loved Him so openly that everyone who knew us, knew we were completely and totally passionate about Him? What if our intellectual pursuits followed our passionate love for Him? In Matthew, we are told that all of God's laws are pegged or hung on this. Our prayers should revolve around this, our lives, desires and wants....all we are should balance or hang on these commands. This is why JOY is defined as Jesus, Others, You! What if our passionate love for God drove our prayers and intellectual pursuits? How can we love You More God? When our minds, hearts and all we desire is centered on Him then and only then will we truly reach the pinnacle of true happiness. Passion, prayer and Intelligence all wrapped up in Him...that's when we arrive. As I walked around the capital of the USA, I saw people from every walk of life including those who were so passionately in love with our country that they gave their very essence of life in military service risking life and losing limbs or more. I felt the extreme love for the country and yet saw the destitution at the foot of the great monuments. I saw these beautiful statues and architecture standing in authentic representation of life and struggle, honor and sentiment but as I watched, I saw many struggles that went untended. I saw a man fall and tumble down the steps of the Lincoln Memorial yet not one person stopped to help him. The bus driver commented on it as we all saw it, yet no one stopped. My heart broke as I imagined God sitting there watching the constant rush but no one willing to lend a hand. The bus pulled over and I got off. I bought a water and went over to this man. I told him to lie still as I helped him drink a little then I called 911. Why? Because it is our duty. It is our charge. It is our humanity. It doesn't matter who he is or why he fell. I could tell you the details but it doesn't matter. He is God's child and we are called to love passionately and fully. I could tell you about my broken foot and all the reasons I shouldn't have gotten off the tour bus but that isn't what it is about. We are called to love passionately, prayerfully and intellectually. I could see his hurt, feel his pain and hear God's heart. Who is in your path today? Are you looking to share His love with passion in prayer and wisdom?

The world is unprincipled. It's dog-eat-dog out there! The world doesn't fight fair. But we don't live or fight our battles that way—never have and never will. The tools of our trade aren't for marketing or manipulation, but they are for demolishing that entire massively corrupt culture. We use our powerful God-tools for smashing warped philosophies, tearing down barriers erected against the truth of God, fitting every loose thought and emotion and impulse into the structure of life shaped by Christ. Our tools are ready at hand for clearing the ground of every obstruction and building lives of obedience into maturity. - 2 Corinthians 10:3-6

Why is it so hard to let Him fight your battles for you?

Are you willing to let him lead you?

Key thought for today:

Fighting Battles?

As I stood watching the changing of the guard, I was impressed by the immense respect and silence. Babies and toddlers that had been fussing minutes earlier suddenly became silent. Hundreds of people stood in awe and respectfully honored those who were guarding the tomb of the unknown man who had given his life for our country. At that moment, it struck my heart deeply that we who had once respectfully honored God for His supreme sacrifice had lost our way. Walking into the halls of that large amphitheater, touring the cases of gifts given in honor, and observing the fort where the soldiers train vigorously for years for the privilege of guarding that grave of the unknown, I learned that the guarding came about because of the disrespect of people. The ceremony that was so awe inspiring and invoked complete respectful silence came about because of disrespect to the tomb. God isn't done with us. 2 Corinthians tells us that this world is unprincipled and a dog-eat-dog world of unfairness and disrespect but we do not operate that way. We do not fight our battles that way. The tools we have are not for sale to use as manipulation or marketing for God but rather for tearing down the corrupt culture of idol selfishness. Our powerful God tools of prayer and anchoring to His word are for tearing down barriers against truth and fitting loose thoughts, emotions and impulses into the life structure He has called us to build. The tools He has given us are ready for us to clear the ground of every obstacle and to build our obedient, mature lives on His foundation. Routines that are trained and ingrained become habits which is why the soldiers train for years to become the guard. They must enact each step meticulously whether a President stands before them or a simple citizen. They must be undeterred from their purpose. They stand guard 24/7 at that tomb in honor of those who gave their lives and never came home or were never identified. The saying says "only God knows" for this is the truth. Science is unable to identify the remains but God knows whose ashes and remains exist within that tomb just as He knows who has admitted His son into their lives. The unknown is a hard place to exist. The why behind a horrible incident of rape, murder, theft, scams, pain, cancer, etc. is a terrible battle but this is why we are called to guard the tomb of the unknown in our hearts. The tomb we guard is that of the old man within us who died not understanding the whys. The guarding is because we must be about the training in our lives to be the person God called us to be and fight our battles on our knees in prayer. I don't know the whys just like I do not know who lies in that tomb. Only God knows. I do know who He is. So I will train and guard my heart and mind, fighting the battles of life as He leads. I don't know about tomorrow but I know Who leads me! If you are tired of fighting against the unknown and are willing to lay it down, He is there willing to fight your battles for you because He knows and He has already won!

God's loyal love couldn't have run out, his merciful love couldn't have dried up.
They're created new every morning. How great your faithfulness!
I'm sticking with God (I say it over and over). He's all I've got left. Lamentations 3:22-24

What is your stickiness? Are you stuck on God until the first wind blows or are you rooted in no matter what?

Key thought for today:

Stuck On God?

As I flew in the plane, gazing out the window, it wasn't hard to fathom the vastness of Earth. When the clouds billow up and surround the plane and you gaze down at that which is usually above, it stretches the mind to embrace His vastness. The newness of His love is more vast and infinite than the clouds formed by droplets of water. His love is so infectious and infinite that it is hard for our minds and hearts to grasp it. His love is not only loyal and never failing but it is so merciful despite our failures and missteps. His faithfulness is constant and this is the why. I love Him because He first loved me but I stick with God despite disappointments because of His faithfulness. When life's trials and tribulations get us down, we have a choice to stick it out trusting that He knows more than we ever could about our circumstances or situations. It is a choice of stubborn love and sticking with it. I love my sticky notes at my office but many of us are like those little notes. We are 1/8th sticky and 7/8th give in/give up/drop out on God. We stick through the good times and we stick through the minor or short duration battles but the tough, we give up on. What is your stickiness? Are you stuck on God until the first wind blows or are you rooted in no matter what? I can promise you that the challenges and tests will come. People will say you have "bad karma" or "God's out to get you" but the truth is just like clouds, life brings rain and storms. God isn't the cause of your storms or situations. He isn't the one who makes bad happen in an imperfect world because this world is full of broken people. He is able to be with you through the storm and He will work things out for your good because that is His promise but your stickiness matters. Slather on the glue of His word, read it, encode it and practice it until it becomes automatic. Stick yourself to His promises and claim them over and over again for His word will not fail and His promises are true. We flew through the clouds and as the mist surrounded us, it was easy to see that it had no substance. The storm may look fierce and seem impossible but with God on board, and you stuck on His promise, you will fly through and the storm will subside with no substance. Greater is He! I am stuck on God! I choose the glue of His word to stick to His promises made with His never failing, everlasting, merciful love. Time to start measuring your stickiness and slathering on His word.

Still later, as the Eleven were eating supper, he appeared and took them to task most severely for their stubborn unbelief, refusing to believe those who had seen him raised up. Then he said, "Go into the world. Go everywhere and announce the Message of God's good news to one and all. Whoever believes and is baptized is saved; whoever refuses to believe is damned. - Mark 16: 14-16

Each of us have the choice and the charge. The choice to believe and the charge to go forth. What will you choose?

Key thought for today:

Is Seeing, Believing?

In Mark, Jesus clearly says that whoever refuses to believe is damned. These are tough words but here He is, Almighty God in the flesh walking around with mortal men and women. He has sacrificed His own life for them and they see Him yet struggle to believe. I have a bucket list of items I want to see in my lifetime but because I haven't seen them doesn't mean I do not believe they exist. God exists in every breath, every dawn, everything in nature and in every cell of our being, yet some still refuse to believe. Like this picture, I have always wanted to see the Northern Lights. It is breathtaking to view the photos and I have no doubt that these lights occur. Belief is a choice. We get this choice. It is a definite choice between God and selfish unbelief which leads to damnation. There are no gray areas or fence sitters. It is a choice: belief or refusal to believe. It isn't a choice of belief or doubt. It is belief in God for who He is or Refusal to believe. Hope, the Eternal Hope comes from belief. Stubborn unbelief prevents us from living the life of The Great Commission to Go everywhere and announce the Message of God's good news to all. Each of us has a different mission field to Go into. Each of us have the choice and the charge. The choice to believe and the charge to go forth. What will we choose?

Everything that goes into a life of pleasing God has been miraculously given to us by getting to know, personally and intimately, the One who invited us to God. The best invitation we ever received! We were also given absolutely terrific promises to pass on to you—your tickets to participation in the life of God after you turned your back on a world corrupted by lust. - 2 Peter 1:3-4

How do we get our tickets to God's promises?

Will you accept your ticket to promise by turning away from that which distracts into that place of submission?

Key thought for today:

Tickets of Promise?

Concerts and events come and people line up to purchase tickets to attend, they get in lotteries and drawings to purchase those that are hard to buy. They purchase the right clothes, the special outfit and accessories to attend. They plan for months or years even but the day comes and then it goes. The event may turn out wonderful or flop but either way, it is over...nothing left but a memory. The best invitation we will ever receive doesn't cost us a dime. It has been miraculously given to us along with everything we need to attend to the pleasing of our hearts and minds. The tickets to God's promises have been issued. The tickets to participate in the life of God come freely after you turn your life and your back on this world corrupted by lust/want/desire/self/flesh. The tickets include Promise and fulfillment on the way to eternal hope in Heaven. The best tickets to the best seats and the best promises are ours. We don't have to participate in a lottery or beg someone to sell them to us. They are ours for the taking by getting to know personally and intimately The One, Jesus who invited us to God. He has prepared and given us all but we must be willing to go with Him by turning away from our own ways. The other day, a small sibling to a client was in the waiting room begging his mom to hurry up to take him to soccer, but as soon as she took his hand to lead him out in the direction he wanted to go, he looked back and saw another child getting some candy. At that moment, he wanted the candy more than to go. This is our sin mindset. It is a fleshly desire for what everyone else has. It is a looking at the other and wanting more instead of putting our hand in His and trusting His best. This my way, right now, or else attitude is not of God but born of sin. When we succumb to this place in our lives, we essentially are saying to God that His tickets of promise in our lives are not good enough. The tickets to promise come with a choice to follow Him. We must fully give our lives and get on the train to eternity but also tell others to come on board with us because He has provided tickets for all! Will you accept your ticket to promise by turning away from that which distracts into that place of submission? It is the absolute best invitation you have ever received!

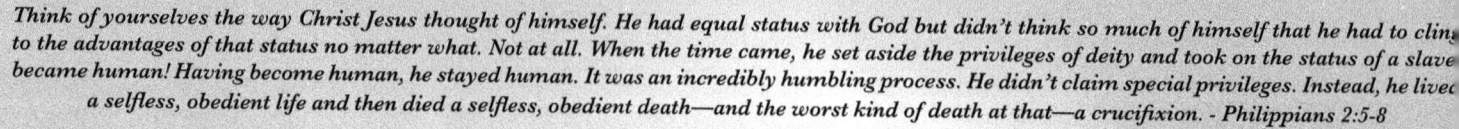

Think of yourselves the way Christ Jesus thought of himself. He had equal status with God but didn't think so much of himself that he had to cling to the advantages of that status no matter what. Not at all. When the time came, he set aside the privileges of deity and took on the status of a slave, became human! Having become human, he stayed human. It was an incredibly humbling process. He didn't claim special privileges. Instead, he lived a selfless, obedient life and then died a selfless, obedient death—and the worst kind of death at that—a crucifixion. - Philippians 2:5-8

Why is status so important to the world?

In the book of Philippians, we are instructed to think of ourselves the way that Christ thought of himself; what does that look like for you?

Key thought for today:

Clinging to Status?

Certain statuses have advantages but those advantages are given by those who award the status. Your status as daughter, mother, sister, wife, etc. is assumed to be rewarded by birth and bloodline but the truth is that these statuses are more than that of blood. They are heart statuses. You can be a daughter by birth but not in action and although you are loved and recognized, if you are not performing the role of daughter, you miss out on the advantages. Today is a special day as my sister celebrates another cycle around the sun. Although we are sisters by blood, it is the heart cycle that matters. I sent her a treat and her office staff videoed it for me. It made my day to see her delight and smile because it reminded me of that heart status that I often miss in the long distance away. Jesus gave His status advantage away when He came to Earth as a newborn babe. He didn't cling to His advantage but rather sacrificed the advantages of that status for us. Our status is not always determined by our roles in life. Many times you can have a role of authority, but perform poorly in that role and lose out because you did not honor those who had given you that status and advantages. In the book of Philippians, we are instructed to think of ourselves the way that Christ thought of himself, for, although he had equal status with God, and all of the advantages that come with that, he chose to sacrifice those advantages rather than cling to those when he came, and offered Himself as a sacrifice for us. His example and role is that we should live a sacrificial life for others. This is often contrary to what the world tells us. The world says take advantage of your status. The world says use all of your advantages for your own benefit. The world says that we should stick up for number one, for ourselves, for what we want. But that is contrary to what Jesus did, and what Jesus says. The real nugget of truth is that the advantages of status come not because we receive salvation through the Lord Jesus Christ, but because we are willing to follow in his example. Salvation comes with the advantage of eternal life. You do not have to do anything other than accept that Jesus Christ is Lord and repent of your sins in order to receive salvation, which leads to eternal life. However, there are things that come through learning to be like Him. Understanding who he is and what the status of being a child of God means, leads to embracing the advantages of a servant heart.

Open your mouth and taste, open your eyes and see—how good God is.
Blessed are you who run to him. - Psalms 34:8

When you have a food craving, what do you most often do to satisfy it?

Does this work the same way in your relationship with God?

Will you stay hungry and doubtful or will you taste and see?

Key thought for today:

Craving Goodness?

If you never open your mouth to taste them you will never know the flavor and goodness of the food put before you. If you never open your eyes, you never will view the beauty and grandeur He has created for us. If you are constantly walking with your eyes on the negative and looking for the bad, you will certainly find it but if you will open your eyes, heart and life to His goodness, it dwells in each day and every moment. The choice is ours to open up. I was craving some homemade enchiladas so I made them. I got the ingredients I needed and put them together perfectly. They were delicious and exactly what I wanted. I also made a pumpkin spice cake with cinnamon cream cheese icing. It was also very yummy. I could tell that both were going to be good by the aromas in my kitchen. Each day, God's fragrance and beauty opens the day. Each morning the sunrise creeps over the sky like a painting by His hands as the birds chirp and the dew settles from the night upon the flowers. The aroma of His love is evident. The psalmist says open your mouth, open your eyes...because it requires us to do the action required to receive what God has for us. First he tells us to open our mouths because God's word is nutritious to our soul. It is a nourishment like no other known as the bread of life and the living water. If we do not open our mouths to His goodness, we cannot experience it. He hasn't left nor taken the food of His love, grace and mercy from us. His fruits of His Spirit surround us but if we are too busy filling ourselves with the other things of life then we miss His nutrients. If we fail to open our eyes to His works and goodness in our lives, then we exist and walk in the disappointments of life. We must celebrate His goodness and His love! We must choose to open our eyes and our mouths to what He has. Recently in a conversation, a person was telling me how bad everything was and how they have nothing to ever look forward to in their life. I told them to look up instead of down. It is a choice. If you look up you will see His light and can swim towards it when you feel like you are drowning but if you are constantly looking at the abyss, then you miss out on His wonders. I understand struggle and I understand loss, pain, and defeat. I get despair and even depression, anxiety and other struggles but I choose each day to taste and see His goodness. I choose to find the good in the struggle despite it all because I know He has worked hard preparing His table for me in the presence of my enemies and He has anointed me in His goodness. All I need to do is open my mouth to taste His goodness and open my eyes to see it. It is a choice. Will you stay hungry and doubtful or will you taste and see? Open your eyes, open your mouth, open your ears, yourself, your heart...open up to Him who has prepared delightful things for your benefit because He loves you with an everlasting love. Look up and Be sweet!

And now, friends, we ask you to honor those leaders who work so hard for you, who have been given the responsibility
of urging and guiding you along in your obedience. Overwhelm them with appreciation and love!
Get along among yourselves, each of you doing your part.- 1 Thessalonians - 5: 12-13

What does honor mean?

Appreciation demonstrates His love to others for their constancy whether we like them or not.
Why do we allow our attitude toward them affect how we treat them?

Isn't it our job to get along with each other, show appreciation and let God judge the right/wrong?
Why do we struggle with this?

Key thought for today:

Honor This?

This weekend for me is a weekend of honoring others. Why? Because we are urged to honor our leaders who have been given the responsibility of urging and guiding us in obedience to God. Sometimes those leaders look differently than expected. My assistant director at my office has been struggling with cancer that suddenly cropped up but without a doubt, she has been the one who urged and encouraged my staff through so much that honoring her and lifting her up is easy. My pastor and his lovely wife along with my parents who serve at their church are due honor for they serve faithfully and consistently. These are easy to honor. But those who are hard to honor are those who do not do exactly as we think they should. Our attitude then is, they are paid for their job just like I am so why should we do more? In Thessalonians, we are urged to show an overwhelming appreciation and love for those who have been given the responsibility of urging us on in obedience and guiding us along that path. Appreciation speaks the language of God's love. Appreciation demonstrates His love to others for their constancy whether we like them or not. Honoring leaders who work hard for us and who have responsibilities to guide us and urge us on is easy when we agree with them but harder when we do not. We can think of a million excuses not to honor them but none of those are in line with God's word. His word instructs us to love our enemies and pray for them. His word instructs us to honor our leaders and show overwhelming appreciation for their service and sacrifice even if we do not agree with them. Honor. Such a concept has been forgotten and replaced with just a word. Honor means to show respect. Honor means to keep an agreement whether you voted them in or not. Politics is a sticky subject because there is such division in opinion. Here is what His word says...Get along among yourselves, each of you doing your part. Overwhelm with appreciation the leaders who have been given the responsibility of urging and guiding you along in obedience. Honor those who work hard in this. It isn't our job to judge whether we should or shouldn't honor, it is our job to get along with each other, show appreciation and let God judge the right/wrong. I promise when we let God be the judge for their labor and not us then things will turn out right. Yes, we must pray, vote, choose wisely but we must also pray, honor and appreciate service whether we like their opinions or not. We do not have to agree with them but we do have to pray for them and honor their service. Today is a day of honor and appreciation specifically for our spiritual leaders. Take the time to overwhelm them with your appreciation!

I'm thanking you, God, from a full heart, I'm writing the book on your wonders.
I'm whistling, laughing, and jumping for joy; I'm singing your song, High God.
- Psalms 9:1-2

What does it look like when your heart is full?

When it seems that you will never get ahead for what you desire or that life is just beating you up, Will you choose gratitude instead of attitude?

Key thought for today:

Full Heart or Empty?

Recently I embarked on a rereading of several great scriptures and reflected again on their power in our lives. While reading again in Psalms 9, this concept jumped out at me. What does a full heart look like? The psalmist describes it as whistling, laughing and jumping for joy. He says he has a full heart as he sings God's song. Being curious, I needed to know what caused his full heart. His full heart comes from understanding who God is. He says "God holds the high center, he sees and sets the world's mess right. He decides what is right for us earthlings, gives people their just deserts" in verse 7. What happens between verse 1 and verse 7? He tells us that his heart is full because God has triumphed against his enemies. This is his testimony time after his test. This is his celebrated moment after he has stood trusting God for the hard and through the tough. His full heart came from worshiping through the trials, through the tests and seeing God triumph. My life has been full of tests lately but I can truly say that when God triumphs in one test and through worshiping, my heart fills up. You cannot fill anything up unless you go to the source. I mean you can siphon gas from a car but it isn't full. You can pour some water from a pitcher to a cup but eventually that pitcher will empty. The only place to get authentic and never ending refreshing to fill your heart is at the source of worship. Your life doesn't have to be perfect to celebrate Him. He has already delivered the winning touchdown, reached the ultimate goal and awarded the prize of the highest calling. Grace. When grace rewrote our story from death to life, we got the reason to testify to His goodness. He passed the test for us with a perfect score. Nothing else really matters and when you go to the source for filling, you realize that No matter what, He is. He is Alpha and Omega, the beginning and the ending. Nothing else truly matters! But on those days when it seems that you will never get ahead for what you desire or that life is just beating you up, try worshiping instead of mully-grubbing. Choose gratitude instead of attitude. Go fill back up in Him and watch how your heart expands with His love. He is enough! Testify to that and watch what He will do!

Everything in the world is about to be wrapped up, so take nothing for granted. Stay wide-awake in prayer. Most of all, love each other as if your life depended on it. Love makes up for practically anything. Be quick to give a meal to the hungry, a bed to the homeless—cheerfully. Be generous with the different things God gave you, passing them around so all get in on it: if words, let it be God's words; if help, let it be God's hearty help. That way, God's bright presence will be evident in everything through Jesus, and he'll get all the credit as the One mighty in everything—encores to the end of time. Oh, yes! - 1 Peter 4:7-11

Scripture gives us these signs and warns us to be vigilant and wide-awake in prayer, "but", Most of all, love each other as if your life depends on it because love makes up for practically anything. How are we to do this and why?

Key thought for today:

End of Time?

Wars and rumors of war, strange earthquakes in diverse places, famine, pestilence and even yet the end has still not come. Skeptics pontificate and scholars ponder but the time of the end draws near as the signs are everywhere. Scripture gives us these signs and warns us to be vigilant and wide-awake in prayer. But the statement that follows is important, it says, Most of all, love each other as if your life depends on it because love makes up for practically anything. Be quick and conscious to give and bless others in love especially those who are hungry and homeless. But don't give of yourself alone, if giving words, guide with God's words and if helping others, give God's heart filled help. God's presence will shine as brightly as this beautiful stream of light from the heavens and He will get all the credit as an encore to His perfect life. Give thanks with a grateful and mindful heart. Jesus is coming soon. Love like that! Pray like that! Take nothing for granted but celebrate everything as His blessings. Watch the end times not in fear but in love for love casts out all fear.

God holds the high center, he sees and sets the world's mess right. He decides what is right for us earthlings, gives people their just deserts. God's a safe-house for the battered, a sanctuary during bad times. The moment you arrive, you relax; you're never sorry you knocked. - Psalms 9:7-10

Jesus at the center of it all. Relax. He's got this. You can just be a support. Won't you choose Him to be your High Center?

Key thought for today:

High Center?

The world is a mess like a mod podge of uncontrolled and uncertain things but God holds the high center and makes it all right with a single move. I remember building a fort out of blankets for my kids, teepees, and other such places to play. There always has to be a core high place to hold the whole thing up, together and prevent a complete collapse. I think of the circus tents. As they are constructing the tent, they know the center will bear the weight and tug of all the other so it must be the strongest. The weight is set. The pole is placed then each of the support posts are measured out from that center. But the tent isn't a tent until that high place is lifted. God says set Him high so He may draw all to Him. The raising high is our life in our choice. God is already the high center of the world He created. He decides what's right for us and He dishes out the rewards or just desserts as He sees fit. God as the high center is a safe house for us during bad times. He is our sanctuary of safety. He always welcomes us and as soon as we arrive in Him, we relax knowing it was the best decision ever. The eye of a hurricane is the quiet place because the closest parts to the eye are the strongest winds. That is the place of rest. That is the place-the eye of the storm. Jesus at the center of it all. Relax. He's got this. You can just be a support. He is the high center. He is the eye. The storm cannot overcome Him.

"Get out of bed, Jerusalem! Wake up. Put your face in the sunlight. God's bright glory has risen for you. The whole earth is wrapped in darkness, all people sunk in deep darkness, But God rises on you, his sunrise glory breaks over you. Nations will come to your light, kings to your sunburst brightness. Look up! Look around! Watch as they gather, watch as they approach you:

Your sons coming from great distances, your daughters carried by their nannies. When you see them coming you'll smile—big smiles! Your heart will swell and, yes, burst! All those people returning by sea for the reunion, a rich harvest of exiles gathered in from the nations! And then streams of camel caravans as far as the eye can see, young camels of nomads in Midian and Ephah, Pouring in from the south from Sheba loaded with gold and frankincense, preaching the praises of God. And yes, a great roundup of flocks from the nomads in Kedar and Nebaioth, Welcome gifts for worship at my altar as I bathe my glorious Temple in splendor. - Isaiah 60:1-7*

Will you choose to be a reflection of His Glory? How?

Key thought for today:

Prophetic Fulfillment?

Instructions for prophetic fulfillment:

• Get out of bed! Often we get into situations where we induce ourselves to sleep by staying in our bed of lies, deceit and sin. It is time to Get out of the Earthly bed of me, me, me.

• Wake Up! Get your thoughts centered on God and not on Earthly things. See His patterns, warnings and signs being fulfilled everywhere!

• Put Your face in the sunlight! God's glory is everywhere if we, but look. When the sun rises, you must face it to see it. We must turn towards God's path and ways in order to see and understand what He is doing and what the signs of the times are saying.

• See God's bright glory risen for you! Quit being a moping mess! God has provided for you and is doing great things for you but you must see it. Not only must you turn towards it but you must recognize and realize what it is that He is doing in your life and the Earth around you.

• Look Up! Quit being downcast and downhearted! You have nothing to be so discouraged about! If you trust in Him, He will surely work it out no matter how bleak it looks. Quit looking at your situation and look up at Him!

• Look Around! The harvest is plenty but the laborers are few. Quit using excuses to sit around and whine about what could be or should be! Turn off that TV and get busy looking for what you can do for His labor. No matter what your situation, you have purpose. You can pray, call, text, email, talk and encourage from your deathbed if needed. Don't waste a minute.

• Watch as they gather! Watch what God is doing. He will bring the need to you when you open your heart. He will bring in those who are ready and you can watch them gather together for His glory.

• Watch as they approach you! Be alert as they approach you! Your family and your spiritual seed is coming to fruition. Watch the growth! See the truth! Know your labor is not in vain.

• Smile big smiles! Your God confirming confidence is attractive and it is contagious! Shine it! Let others see His love shine through your smile!

• Welcome! Invite, excite and then welcome the roundups of harvest as they pour into you! God has prepared you! It is now your job to be ready to welcome them to the kingdom of God.

In this all-out match against sin, others have suffered far worse than you, to say nothing of what Jesus went through—all that bloodshed! So don't feel sorry for yourselves. Or have you forgotten how good parents treat children, and that God regards you as his children? My dear child, don't shrug off God's discipline, but don't be crushed by it either. It's the child he loves that he disciplines; the child he embraces, he also corrects. God is educating you; that's why you must never drop out. He's treating you as dear children. This trouble you're in isn't punishment; it's training, the normal experience of children. Only irresponsible parents leave children to fend for themselves. Would you prefer an irresponsible God? We respect our own parents for training and not spoiling us, so why not embrace God's training so we can truly live? While we were children, our parents did what seemed best to them. But God is doing what is best for us, training us to live God's holy best. At the time, discipline isn't much fun. It always feels like it's going against the grain. Later, of course, it pays off big-time, for it's the well-trained who find themselves mature in their relationship with God.
Hebrews 12:4-11.

God is educating us and it isn't punishment but discipline. Would you prefer an irresponsible God?
How can we embrace the training and discipline in moments of hard circumstances with a positive attitude?

What is the long term benefit of enduring this "training"?

Key thought for today:

Well Trained?

Training is what I do. Specifically in my specialty it is brain training or cognitive therapy but essentially helping people learn to learn more easily and to help the brain do what it needs to do. Training requires discipline. This isn't always fun but pays off in the end. This is an all out match against sin. God is educating us and it isn't punishment but discipline. Would you prefer an irresponsible God? We need to embrace the training even through it because this is how we grow. God is training us to live God's holy best. During the training, it can be hard but we must endure for it pays off in the long term. I have been blessed this week to meet up with former clients who are doctors and lawyers, politicians, plumbers and even a judge. All of these came into my life because of a struggle in their own lives but they were willing to embrace the discomfort of the discipline and training of their brain in order to get long term gains. It paid off for them as it always does. Training and discipline equal long term benefits whether it be physical, mental, spiritual or emotional. Well trained people become mature in God's manners. Well trained people embrace discipline and challenges. Look at your situation as a training ground to become the best holy you that God can make. He is refining us, proving us, molding us and perfecting us for His glory. God is not an irresponsible God as many parents are. He knows that as hard as this is, you will thrive as you embrace the discipline of this moment. Learn to embrace it as a time of becoming the best you. No matter what your circumstances. The best is yet to come! Get busy training!

God's glory is on tour in the skies, God-craft on exhibit across the horizon.
Madame Day holds classes every morning, Professor Night lectures each evening.
Psalms 19:1-2

What is He calling you to attend to? What classes or lectures is He signing you up for? What purpose has He given to you?

What is on the horizon for us to learn from Him?

Key thought for today:

God-Craft?

First a warning: this word is going to challenge you because it is easy to be defensive when you are stuck in a place. Someone asked me to "review" as in listen or read a book on spells in witchcraft. My immediate reaction was no, that isn't of God so stay far away. Then I heard a quiet voice telling me this was an opportunity to reach into the dark for one of His lost lambs. I gotta say I am a scaredy cat. I do not like dark places, scary movies, etc. I decided to seek God to see if this was really a place He wanted me to step into. As I was praying, this verse-this exact translation came to my heart. God is on tour and He is showing His God-craft around the world, across the skies and throughout the horizons. God is instructive day and night. He creates beauty and sends messages but we are slow to see them and eager to just live in the realm of Earthly existence without reaching to understand the spiritual implications. Pride and ungratefulness are said to be worse than witchcraft by the Word and yet we live in both of these daily, dwelling there and forgetting whose we are. Madame Day and Professor Night holding classes and lectures is a lot easier to interpret than "The heavens declare the glory of God; And the firmament shows His handiwork."
Psalms 19:1 NKJV. It is all about interpretation and Spirit. The Rainbow is a symbol. Originally it was set as a promise from God. Others have decided to use it to represent other promises such as the rainbow bridge when someone loses a pet, the rainbow baby which is a child born after child loss, and the rainbow finance which is the pot of gold from investment. "Somewhere Over The Rainbow" is a favorite classic song to indicate we are all in this world together. And some pernicious groups have attached the rainbow to their cause thinking it represents them. This is the battle of life-the light/dark. This is where He instructs us by day and by night. God's glory is on tour in the skies. What is He calling you to attend to? What classes or lectures is He signing you up for? What purpose has He given to you? I do not always like my lessons but I do learn. God-craft versus witchcraft. I know which is more powerful. I know who holds tomorrow and I know who the Master of all classes, the Dean, the Head of Schools for this tour is. What is on the horizon for us to learn from Him?

"I don't think the way you think. The way you work isn't the way I work." God's Decree. "For as the sky soars high above earth, so the way I work surpasses the way you work, and the way I think is beyond the way you think. Just as rain and snow descend from the skies and don't go back until they've watered the earth, Doing their work of making things grow and blossom, producing seed for farmers and food for the hungry, So will the words that come out of my mouth not come back empty-handed. They'll do the work I sent them to do, they'll complete the assignment I gave them.
Isaiah 55:8-11

God's word is set and will not return void but what if we as a people could stand up in the gap, being the difference, changing and moving the mind and heart of God towards our country instead of against it because of our willful ways and ignorance? What if we who are the people He cares so deeply for can turn His hand in love instead of anger towards us? What if we could be the difference?

How can I know the will of God and seek to move His heart at the same time?

Key thought for today:

Assignments Completed?

As we watched the eclipse yesterday, we all were amazed by something set into the celestial calendar by God once spoken with four simple words millions of years ago. Let there be Light! God's decree is beyond our wildest imagination and yet, His hand and word can be moved by us. I love the story of Esther as tragic as it is because it is an allegory to our story. Esther was born as Hadassah. Hadassah is a Hebrew girl's name meaning "myrtle tree". Symbolically, the myrtle tree is associated with peace, love, and prosperity. Queen Esther of Persia is noted for her faithful devotion to God and her sweet, docile nature in history but her life was not an easy one. First, her parents died, then she was kidnapped and child trafficked to be the plaything of a king in a foreign country. She wasn't pampered because she was of royal birth. She was forced to undergo horrible things to adapt to a king's appetite because he was a drunken lush who cast his wife away. God had purpose and favor on her but at the time, it sure didn't feel like that! The way He worked in her life was for the purpose of saving the Jewish people from annihilation but as a young girl, I feel sure she was confused and hurt that she felt God wasn't hearing her prayers. Rain, snow, sun, wind, hurricane, and other weather events both beautiful, Necessary, and frightening at times all are a part of His plans. The way He works has purpose. So here is this young lady who has now caught the eye of the king, become the queen despite all the horror and now she finds herself in a quandary. Will she be used as an instrument of God's hand and for His purpose to save His people? The Jewish holiday of Purim is to celebrate her willingness to step into that gap and be the salvation of her people by staying the hand of the king. She couldn't stop what he had already decreed as it was law but she was able to change the mind of the king and he was moved by her request and her constancy to write a new law which protected the Jewish people in this foreign land. God's word is set and will not return void but what if we as a people could stand up in the gap, being the difference, changing and moving the mind and heart of God towards our country instead of against it because of our willful ways and ignorance? What if we could be "The people called by His name" who humble themselves in prayer, praise and repentance to He who has the ability and authority to decree? What if we could be the ones who take what the enemy meant for evil and turn it for good by imploring the will of God to heal our land and use us for His glory? What if we complete the assignment we were sent to do for such a time as this? The eclipse has a purpose, set in motion millions of years ago but Joshua prayed for the sun to stand still in battle and it did. What if? He has called you, purposed you, provided for you and you are His. We are His people and He cares about us. What if we who are the people He cares so deeply for can turn His hand in love instead of anger towards us? What if we could be the difference? Esther risked it all as she approached the king's court. It was the law that if she was not accepted or received his favor that she would be banned and killed. She prepared in her chamber both mentally, physically and spiritually then she went into his presence to turn his heart towards her people. Today, we have the opportunity to stand up, prepare our hearts, minds and bodies for His will and to approach His throne in supplication for our country. Today we can turn the heart of God towards us by going into His Holy of Holies, behind the hidden veil, where He as the Most High dwells. We go with the opportunity to change His heart towards us but we must first humble ourselves to seek His word and His will so we know His plan. How can I know the will of God and seek to move His heart at the same time? His will is listed in His word. His promises and decrees are already set just as the eclipse millions of years ago by His word that does not return void. We know Him and He loves us. If My people....time to complete His assignment for us.

"Don't look for shortcuts to God. The market is flooded with surefire, easygoing formulas for a successful life that can be practiced in your spare time. Don't fall for that stuff, even though crowds of people do The way to life—to God!—is vigorous and requires total attention. - Matthew 7:13-14

What is the formula to solving the problem of life?

The tests of life come in all sizes, shapes and durations. What is the key to overcoming and walking through them?

Key thought for today:

Surefire Formula?

I sat with her practicing the test but she was struggling to remember the formula she needed. It wasn't locked into her mind because she didn't use it enough to have it be automatically ingrained. She kept wanting me to give her a hint, a shortcut, or the answer but my role was not to do that but to help her learn the right method to solving the problem. The formula to solving the problem of life is by embracing who God is and seeking His direction at each step. Putting His words in your heart memory so when the test pressure is on, the recall of His promise is instant. The tests of life are real and constant but the Promises of God, alive and vibrant in His word, stand the tests of time. There is no problem too big that God cannot solve it. There is no challenge too hard for Him nor a situation too tough that He cannot remove it. We must stop the work arounds and shortcuts such as a fixed little ditty or song for our prayers and learn that God is not a formula or shortcut. He is life itself. We cannot just microwave our issues into complete solutions without Him. This just creates more problems down the road. The way through is to learn the promises by heart and to walk in them through the tests. The tests of life come in all sizes, shapes and durations. Embracing them is the way to understanding who He is. Walking through the trial with Him and quoting His promises is the proof. He demonstrated this for us with His life and His death and His resurrection. Death isn't too big for Him and Life is full of trials and temptations that we overcome by the power of the Word and our testimony. Solving the problem requires knowing the how, not the why the author wrote the problem or put it on the test. Simply heart memory of who He is and that His word is the key/the formula/the secret/the solution. She learned to learn from me. She learned the formulas by heart but mostly she learned how to solve problems on a test by eliminating those distractions and wrong answers so the true answer is revealed. God wants us to learn from Him that same principle. The way to life is vigorous and requires us to pay total attention to what He is doing and not get distracted by the fake or false information and strategies flooding through life as the tips to success. The success formula is non-existent without God. There isn't a mindset nor a principle nor a trick/tip that exists to shortcut our life nor the pathway to Him. You must learn to learn His ways and His promises and lean into His truths. Shortcuts lead to other problems and away from who He is. "In all your ways, acknowledge Him and He will direct your path."

God will order a blessing on your barns and workplaces;
he'll bless you in the land that God, your God, is giving you.
All the peoples on Earth will see you living under the
Name of God and hold you in respectful awe. - Deuteronomy 28:8,10

Blessing is a powerful thing and living in blessings is even more so.
What would happen if we began to walk in blessings only?

What if we follow Him without question or doubt, did as He commanded and stood for only that which was right?

How are we walking? In the shadow of the moon or in the promise of the Son?

Key thought for today:

Ordered Blessings?

Deuteronomy is one of the books of law in the Bible. In this particular chapter, Moses is speaking the promises of God over the people if they keep God's commandments. We love verses like this for they are life, encouragement and a breath of fresh air in troubled times. Just know that this is but one of the promises that is available to us IF we keep His commands. My pastor has been preaching on the IFs at church. IF is a powerful word of choice. We have a choice. You see this promise doesn't say that God did order a blessing, it says He will order the blessing IF. It is a choice to follow His ways or your own. It is a choice to do as He directs, be grateful for His provision and move in Him or to go our own way. His blessings or His curse. If you continue to read in this chapter, the curse is something fierce. The curse is a lot of what we see the Israelites go through in the Biblical stories because they made poor choices as a people. I cannot help but wonder if there were some within that people group who lived in blessing while watching those around them living in a curse all because of choices. I cannot help but wonder if the whole of Israel had at least one family who walked in blessing during their times of trial as a people because they chose to follow His ways despite the others around them. Blessing is a powerful thing and living in blessings is even more so. What would happen if we began to walk in blessings only? What if we follow Him without question or doubt, did as He commanded and stood for only that which was right? This scripture tells us what would happen. God will order a blessing for us in providing for us and in our homes, workplaces, land, and country. It says everyone will see us living under the Name of God and hold us in respectful awe! I for one am claiming this promise in my life. God, I ask you to order a blessing on my behalf as I walk in your ways and commands. I want to live in your blessings and promises not in a life of curses and pain. I know that even in a life of blessings, problems arise to test that life but I want to walk in your promises despite the struggles, confident that you are working all things out for my good. I thank you for these promises and ask for you to order the blessings down on me. How are we walking? In the shadow of the moon or in the promise of the Son? You may feel like you are in the shadow for a moment of life, but remember that eclipses happen in life. They don't hide the Son for long and they cannot stop His ordered blessings and favor. Remember even if we are currently in shadow to continue to walk in His promise of blessing according to His commandments because the eclipse is passing and His storehouse of blessings can be ours for the asking. If. It is our choice.

Thank God! Call out his Name! Tell the whole world who he is and what he's done! Sing to him! Play songs for him! Broadcast all his wonders! Revel in his holy Name, God-seekers, be jubilant! Study God and his strength, seek his presence day and night; Remember all the wonders he performed, the miracles and judgments that came out of his mouth. Seed of Israel his servant! Children of Jacob, his first choice! He is God, our God; wherever you go you come on his judgments and decisions. He keeps his commitments across thousands of generations, the covenant he commanded, The same one he made with Abraham, the very one he swore to Isaac; He posted it in big block letters to Jacob, this eternal covenant with Israel: "I give you the land of Canaan, this is your inheritance; Even though you're not much to look at, a few straggling strangers." - 1 Chronicles 16:8-19

Why do we need to study God?

What are some of the ways that you find helpful to studying God?

Key thought for today:

Studying God?

In Chronicles, we are instructed to study God. How do we go about this and why? The why comes first. We study God to know who He is. You cannot serve someone well without knowing them. You cannot be a true part of someone in a relationship without knowing them. You cannot tell others about someone until you know them and understand who they are. The instructions to why/how to study God are given in easy steps.

• Thank God for what He has done. If you don't know, it is because you haven't looked around you in wonder at the works of His hands. Start looking at the smallest flower, the tiniest birds, the intricacies of His creation, and the works of His hands.

• Call out His name! The power in His name calms storms, heals the blind and makes the dead alive again. You learn this from studying His word.

• Tell the world who He is and what He's done. That's called bragging rights to who He is. Read the stories and retell them because then they become ingrained in your heart. When you recount what He has done, then you affirm what great and mighty things He will do in you and for you.

• Sing to Him! Play songs for Him! This is worship because the power of praise is the mightiest thing on Earth. If you study what it does and has done, you will know how great He is. Songs and shouts of praise cause demons to tremble, walls to fall down, prisons to open and miracles to happen and so much more. The power of praise is the mightiest refrain as it carries the current of change.

• Broadcast all His wonders! You cannot talk about it loudly and proudly unless you know about it. Studying His word allows you to tell about the times He did mighty things. These reaffirmations put you in the right frame of mind during your times of trials and tests.

• Revel in His Holy Name! God-seekers, be jubilant! This one means to choose joy and happiness during your trials and tests. This type of knowing and celebrating during the tough times takes God confidence that only comes from studying Him and His words.

• Know His strength. The same God who raised Jesus from the grave dwells in us, lives in us. The same power that caused the Red Sea to part to become dry land lives in us. The same power that caused the blind to see and the lame to walk lives in us. There is nothing mightier than He, the power in His name causes mountains to move and the dead to live.

• Seek His presence day and night! The seeking causes a yearning, a strong desire to know more of who He is. The more you seek Him, the more you will find and the more you find, the more you will love about Him. The depth of relationship with Him comes from the seeking which leads to the knowing and the knowing to the depth of understanding of His love and who He is.

• Remember the wonders he performed and the miracles and judgements that came from His mouth. Put them in memory by recounting them and reciting them. There, you will have easy access to knowing Him.

• Know His promises are true and forever. Things change. Life changes. Land changes. Winds change. Circumstances change. God never changes. His promises do not change. His word is forever. His truth is abundant and solid. He isn't subject to political pressure nor to a whim of kings, rulers or leaders of countries. He is God.

• He is God! Wherever you go, you will come upon His judgments and His decisions. He is forever. He keeps His commitments across thousands of generations. He keeps the covenants He commands. The same promises He swore millions of years ago, He adheres to always. He has eternal covenants with Israel that we must adhere to and understand. Study God! Study to show yourself approved as a workman worthy of hiring. Study to pass life's tests. Study God for only then can you understand your place and your purpose. Happiness is knowing God. You cannot know Him unless you study Him.

"Afflicted city, storm-battered, unpitied: I'm about to rebuild you with stones of turquoise, Lay your foundations with sapphires, construct your towers with rubies, Your gates with jewels, and all your walls with precious stones. All your children will have God for their teacher— what a mentor for your children! You'll be built solid, grounded in righteousness, far from any trouble—nothing to fear! far from terror—it won't even come close! If anyone attacks you, don't for a moment suppose that I sent them, And if any should attack, nothing will come of it. I create the blacksmith who fires up his forge and makes a weapon designed to kill. I also create the destroyer— but no weapon that can hurt you has ever been forged. Any accuser who takes you to court will be dismissed as a liar. This is what God's servants can expect.
I'll see to it that everything works out for the best." God's Decree. - Isaiah 54:11-17

Can you remember a time when God's word came to you and was just what you needed to hear?
How did that moment affect you and your situation?

Is there a certain promise that you cling to when you are in the midst of a storm?

Key thought for today:

Storm Battered?

My tiredness caught me by surprise. My body knew, my husband knew, but the true fatigue was hidden from me by adrenaline. I had been working long hours pouring out in high emotional situations and my heart was exhausted. Then I went to the rebuilder. Oh How sweet it is that He knows exactly what we need to hear. We are jewels in His eyes. Highly valued and precious, He desires us to be fully appreciated. Polishing stone and cutting it so the true beauty is beheld, it's hard on the stone but the master jeweler knows exactly what He is doing. In Isaiah, this promise of His to Jerusalem is also ours. He promises to rebuild us with jewels. He promises to be the teacher for our children and that although attacks in life will come, we will not be harmed. He promises that accusers will be put aside and everything will come out best for us. We often quote part of this verse as no weapon built against me will prosper as that is what it says. But we forget the true jewel hidden under it all. The beautiful rebuilding of our lives doesn't just lie in this gorgeous tower of rubies and foundations of sapphire but in the promise that He Himself will see to it that all things work together for good for those who love Him and serve Him. All things, not some things. All things. Look at the stormed out place of fatigue in your life and know with confidence that God is rebuilding that exact place in life into a beautiful thing. It may look like a cut up, muddy mess right now but that is because the Master Jeweler has us under construction. We are a people under construction because God isn't complete with us. We may feel like an afflicted, storm-battered mess, but God has us in His construction plan with the foundation being reset with sapphires and the towers of power built with rubies. He is working beautiful things from our ashes. Rest. Go rest in Him knowing that your labor has purpose and all things are working on your behalf.

"But down the road the population of Israel is going to explode past counting, like sand on the ocean beaches. In the very place where they were once named Nobody, they will be named God's Somebody. Everybody in Judah and everybody in Israel will be assembled as one people. They'll choose a single leader. There'll be no stopping them—a great day in Jezreel!" - Hosea 1:10-11

What was the reason for God to have Hosea name his children Jezreel, Lo-Ruhamah (No-Mercy) and Lo-Ammi (Nobody)?

Spend some time today thanking God for His mercy.

Key thought for today:

Who Are You?

I have to admit that Hosea was a unique guy who definitely had a heart for God. The first chapter of Hosea is a little hard to swallow. First, God is mad at Israel for being unfaithful and so He decides to use Hosea to understand the way God feels by making his life an

example. He tells him to marry a promiscuous woman, a prostitute. He does. They have three

children whom God has named. First a son, Jezreel, because God is angry at how they massacred the people there. Then a daughter, named No-Mercy because God is expressing that He is angry and will show no mercy for their unfaithfulness then another son named Nobody.

Why this matters so much is because in this single chapter we see God directing a whole nation in the same manner as He is directing this family. He tells Hosea to marry a prostitute and love her unconditionally despite her unfaithful behavior to him because that is how God loves us. He names the children after the feelings He redeems. Jezreel reminds us we are never forgotten. No Mercy becomes an example of God's infinite mercy and Nobody becomes God's Somebody. As I sat at a luncheon yesterday, I visited with parents of children who had come to my center as children feeling like nobody because they struggled with learning issues and through brain training they learned they were somebody special. I listened as their parents told me of their successes, two doctors, one lawyer and one a teacher. I thought then how

wonderful it was that God took a little girl who felt unimportant and was told often by others that she was a nobody, to reach others who felt like nobodies so they could become somebodies. No matter what happens in life, we are God's Somebody and that is more important than the biggest title, highest position of power and largest bank account. He knows my name. He sees my heart. He uses every part of me for His purpose. I am a Nobody to others but to the only one who matters, I am His Somebody.

Friends love through all kinds of weather,
and families stick together in all kinds of trouble.
Proverbs 17:17

What's the difference between stuck and sticky?

Spend some time today being thankful for those who are there for you when you get "sticky".

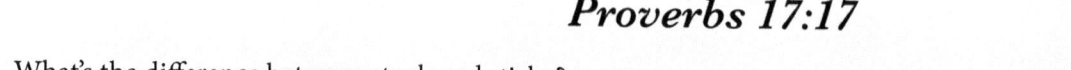

Key thought for today:

Stuck or Sticky?

These last few days I have waffled in being stuck in one place with a lot of muck but I have been so very grateful for friends and family who have helped me by being sticky. What's the difference between stuck and sticky? Stuck is unmoving and often is like a rut we cannot move from but sticky is a place of touchpoint. A sticky note sticks to a surface as long as needed but when removed leaves no residue or evidence of it being there. This kind of sticky is referred to in Proverbs as the kind of sticky we need. Friends love no matter what and families are there as needed...backbone. I am so grateful for my friends and family. I am so blessed to have them in my life. Life isn't always perfect and sometimes we go through things that leave us feeling stuck in a rut but the truth is that God surrounds us with people who can help us become unstuck with their sticky stubborn love that comes from Him. I am thankful for the truth talks and the truth walks from friends and family. You may not always know who is seeing you and knowing what you do but just keep walking and keep talking about His love because I promise, you are seen, you are needed and you are loved!

"What am I doing in the meantime, Lord? Hoping, that's what I'm doing—hoping You'll save me from a rebel life, save me from the contempt of idiots. I'll say no more, I'll shut my mouth, since you, Lord, are behind all this. But I can't take it much longer. When you put us through the fire to purge us from our sin, our dearest idols go up in smoke. Are we also nothing but smoke? - Psalms 39:7-11

What are we doing? Are we achieving purpose?

What happens when we get our mind fixed on the promises? The hope?

Key thought for today:

What Am I Doing?

In the meantime, the meanwhile, the time before, the now, what am I doing? Hoping. Hoping God will save me from the rebellious streak in me and from the contempt of others. Oh how David had the words I feel so often. What are we doing? When God puts us through our fiery tests to purge us and burns up those things that keep us from Him, do we also become smoke? Are we but vapors in the wind, fog upon the ground? What are we doing? Are we achieving purpose? In conversations the last few days, I've spoken with so many who are tired of the waiting, fatigued in the fields, tired of the toil, but still going. Some are tired of fighting illness or disease while living in hope for a better place; some are in career change or challenges and wishing that the waiting place would hurry up; some are just feeling the age of life and the turmoil of the world and the hope or longing for more is wearing. Hope. What are we doing? We are walking in the hope of His soon return. We are walking in the hope of His promises. We are waking each day confident that He is who He says He is and that His words are truth and life. Why? Because, the what am I doing gets to be a burden unless we hold onto the hope. When we get our mind fixed on the promises and fixed on the hope, then we can walk in the praise which unlocks the power of the hope promise. Then, what am I doing becomes a praise of who He is instead of a why am I here. The negative mindset and frustration with the truth and burdens of life get lost in the wonders of His love and goodness. Think about His love. Think about His goodness. Think about His grace that has brought you through. Think about the miracles He has done. Think about it and testify of it because the power of praise is the change that ignites the bonfire of hope into His promises. When we focus on the "what am I doing in the meantime", we get bogged down. We cling to hope like a life raft in an ocean but when we begin to focus on His goodness, love and mercy to us, the hope ignites into praise which tears down those walls of self-pity and ignites the eternal flame of promise that He has for us. David experienced this. These words are from chapter 39 but then hope ignited and he wrote these words in chapter 40- "Blessed are you who give yourselves over to God, turn your backs on the world's "sure thing," ignore what the world worships; The world's a huge stockpile of God-wonders and God-thoughts. Nothing and no one compares to you! I start talking about you, telling what I know, and quickly run out of words. Neither numbers nor words account for you." Psalms 40:4-5 MSG Nothing compares to God. No one, no thing! Start talking about Him, tell what you know and then the flame of hope ignites the promises He has given for us. Get your mind off things of this world and get your mind on Him. Ignite His promises in your life. Red in the morning is a sailor's warning but red at night is their delight. The red is there in our lives. We can choose whether it's the morning or the night. We can choose to rest in Him or ready ourselves to fight it alone. What am I doing in the meantime? I am hoping in the Lord and singing His praises to ignite the promises He has given in His word.

But all who are hunting for you— oh, let them sing and be happy.
Let those who know what you're all about tell the world you're great and not quitting.
And me? I'm a mess. I'm nothing and have nothing: make something of me.
You can do it; you've got what it takes— but God, don't put it off. - Psalms 40:16-17

Are you willing to be broken and put back together to become a masterpiece for God?

Are you willing to become a vessel of His choosing, pouring out His love on others?

Key thought for today:

And Me?

These beautiful roses in all their grandeur are hard to see in detail behind the scripture unless your eyes search to see them. I love participating in those find the letter/number/shape/difference type of visual processing games. As a brain trainer, I know not only do these intrigue me and keep my brain active and growing but also they help the brain form new neural networks. It is in the hunting that the value is found, not just in the winning. It is in the process. The psalmist knows this as he encourages us to hunt for God. He knows the hunting leads to the praise and the happiness/joy of song in your heart. I remember my grandma always had a song in her heart that she was humming or singing under her breath constantly. The song and message we should be singing is about how great He is through everything. God is great. He doesn't quit. He's an on time God. Me? I'm a mess just like this psalmist. I'm nothing and have nothing of importance but Him. God, I ask you like the psalmist did to make me into something like you. I want to be a masterpiece even if it takes being broken. You have all that is needed, all that it takes to make me like you God. Don't wait. Don't put it off. Make me your vessel, an offering of love. Use me for your glory. Help me to humbly be what you desire me to be. God, I am hunting for you. I want to sing for joy and tell the world of your amazing feats, blessings and honors. Make me your vessel. Make me your offering. Make me whatever you want me to be.

God's readiness to give and forgive is now public. Salvation's available for everyone!
We're being shown how to turn our backs on a godless, indulgent life, and how to take on a God-filled, God-honoring life.
This new life is starting right now, and is whetting our appetites for the glorious day when our great God and Savior, Jesus Christ, appears. He offered himself as a sacrifice to free us from a dark, rebellious life into this good, pure life, making us a people he can be proud of, energetic in goodness. - Titus 2:11-14

Which balloon are you? Did you fill up, close off and now you are on the dying drift or are you finally free in Him to go where He takes you, fuels you and transporting others with you?

Key thought for today:

Feeling Energetic?

I work with kids all day long and they have so much energy that sometimes they make me tired just watching them. One precious little redhead yesterday was feeling especially vivid and vibrant so I asked her about why she was so excited. Her answer, "because I am happy. Happiness makes you just wanna jump and holler." That is when I had an epiphany. Happiness is not only our choice but our lifestyle, our demonstration and our witness. Happiness comes from joy and is vibrant. Happiness is energetic in goodness. God's readiness to give to us and forgive us is public. We should be walking billboards of His goodness and graciousness. We should be bubbling over with gratitude and excitement that we have a home filled with wonderful things, instead most of us walk around like we are beat down and lost, saying " I cannot wait for God to come back because this world is so terrible." Why? Why would a person who doesn't know Jesus want to join a parade of sorrow and poor me? We are made more than conquering warriors through Jesus. We are promised a home prepared for us in Heaven. We aren't "just passing through"; we are here on a mission. We have purpose. We need to get our minds off our Earthly means and problems and remember who we are in Him. We are shown how to turn our backs on our self-indulgent life so we can be God filled and God honoring in our lives. What is the difference in a helium balloon and a hot air balloon? One takes all it can hold, shuts off, floats a while then loses air and is done for. One takes on a constant fuel until it catches the wind of God and then it rises above, taking with it those around so that their eyes travel upward continuously and constantly. The basket that is attached carries others with them to new places and new heights. Which balloon are you? Did you fill up, close off and now you are on the dying drift or are you finally free in Him to go where He takes you, fuels you and transporting others with you? Whet your appetite! He came to release us from the beat down path of the law and from that dark, rebellious life into a good, free, pure life we can be proud of, full of energy and goodness. Quit looking down at the ground! Look up! This new lifestyle full of God's energy can be yours today! I am choosing energetic happiness!

It wasn't so long ago that we ourselves were stupid and stubborn, easy marks for sin, ordered every which way by our glands, going around with a chip on our shoulder, hated and hating back. But when God, our kind and loving Savior God, stepped in, he saved us from all that. It was all his doing; we had nothing to do with it. He gave us a good bath, and we came out of it new people, washed inside and out by the Holy Spirit. Our Savior Jesus poured out new life so generously. God's gift has restored our relationship with him and given us back our lives. And there's more life to come—an eternity of life! You can count on this. I want you to put your foot down. Take a firm stand on these matters so that those who have put their trust in God will concentrate on the essentials that are good for everyone. Stay away from mindless, pointless quarreling over genealogies and fine print in the law code. That gets you nowhere. Warn a quarrelsome person once or twice, but then be done with him. It's obvious that such a person is out of line, rebellious against God. By persisting in divisiveness he cuts himself off. - Titus 3:8-11

Are we any more righteous than the worst among us?

What will you choose; to live your life as an example of truth and God's love, which sees the sin and is willing to bathe it in His love, to allow Him to wash you clean, or will you just sit back and allow the stench to remain upon you?

Key thought for today:

Bathed in Love?

Stupid, stubborn sin keeps us filthy until we are able to finally realize that we need a good bath in his love. My puppy really wanted to sit by me on the couch but his stench was overwhelming! I was very tired but he was in need of a good bath and whining to sit with me, so I got myself up and bathed him in a good smelling shampoo and then loved on him with a towel until he was dry and feeling pampered. He got up close to me on the couch and I could still smell the stench. After investigating, I realized that although I had washed his fur, I hadn't taken into account his breath. He was washed on the outside but the inside was still reeking of whatever he had gotten into. This is us. God is there constantly loving on us but our stench comes from inside and we have to be bathed wholly inside and out to erase the stench of sin to be covered in His loving grace that opens the windows of Heaven to us. In Titus, we are reminded that we are driven easily into our own ways of sin and stench, stubbornness and stupidity, walking around with chips on our shoulders, hating others and being hated. But when we allow or moreover choose to step into the bath of God's love, we are washed not only outside but inside completely as a new person. This life He poured out into us is a new life with a fresh smell and a fresh renewal so that we are clean throughout. This gift of love restores our relationship and gives us back the life He had intended for us all along before sin stole our purpose. What we must do is put our foot down and take a firm stand on righteousness. We must stay away from pointless quarrels on things that do not matter. Arguing over your opinion of things is purposeless. It doesn't win friends nor convince others to serve God. It only alienates them to the point that they avoid all contact with you then you lose the right to speak truth into their lives. I do not agree with certain lifestyles and I see that sin besets others. I choose to live my life as an example of truth and God's love which sees the sin and is willing to bathe it in His love to allow Him to wash them clean. I am not the Savior, only a humble servant assisting in running the bath water of His love and holding the towel to support them after they are bathed. Bathing is a continuous process because just like my puppy, we are all sinners who too often decide to run back into the places of sin in our lives that we have not allowed to be fully washed. There is none righteous, no, not one. You are as dirty as I and just as much in need of a Savior's bath of love as the worst among us. Sin is sin. Dirt is dirt. Whether it is caked on mud and just some dust from carelessly living, we all need to be bathed in His love continually. Quit judging and get busy running the bath water instead!

"I'm telling you these things while I'm still living with you. The Friend, the Holy Spirit whom the Father will send at my request, will make everything plain to you. He will remind you of all the things I have told you. I'm leaving you well and whole. That's my parting gift to you. Peace. I don't leave you the way you're used to being left—feeling abandoned, bereft. So don't be upset. Don't be distraught.
"You've heard me tell you, 'I'm going away, and I'm coming back.' If you loved me, you would be glad that I'm on my way to the Father because the Father is the goal and purpose of my life. - John 14:25-28

How do you describe peace?

Who is The Friend that Jesus left us with? What is the purpose of this Friend?

Key thought for today:

Peaceful?

Gentle Spirit touch this world filled with ache and woe.
Turn hearts and minds toward our Father we should know.
Special Friend, one of a kind, sent to remind us of Him.
Be our guide, close by our sides as we seek His gems.
Make plain to our hearts with no doubt or fuss
that we are made for purpose.
Remind us of His loving ways so we may achieve His glory daze.

Peace. It is a gift like no other. It is the gift of comfort in times of turmoil and angst. It is a knowing in the confusion and a certainty in the uncertain. Peace isn't about the storm. Peace is being well and whole despite the storm. It is absolute confidence in the face of the unknown. But Peace is a gift that was left by Jesus for us through acceptance of The Friend, The Holy Spirit. The Friend is here always speaking peace and safety but we must listen and remember our purpose. If we stray away from the purpose, we can no longer hear and feel the gift of peace. It is a carry with you gift but because the Spirit is of God and is God, He will not enter into places and things that are not of Him unless it is His purpose or calling to do so. The Holy Spirit, our friend, is here for the express purpose of reminding us of what Jesus taught and to draw us continually back to God's purpose. The Father is the goal and purpose. Not anything more than Him. Peace in the midst of trouble, in the storm, in the shaking and quaking of life comes from the confidence of the knowing. That still small voice in your head remains to remind you of who He is and what His purpose is in us. It is called intuition or foreknowledge or insight or by many other names but Jesus said it is The Friend, The Holy Spirit. Goal and Purpose in line equals peace. Know Peace, Know God. No Peace, No God and vice versa as they are one and the same.

" "When a woman gives birth, she has a hard time, there's no getting around it. But when the baby is born, there is joy in the birth. This new life in the world wipes out memory of the pain. The sadness you have right now is similar to that pain, but the coming joy is also similar. When I see you again, you'll be full of joy, and it will be a joy no one can rob from you. You'll no longer be so full of questions. "This is what I want you to do: Ask the Father for whatever is in keeping with the things I've revealed to you. Ask in my name, according to my will, and he'll most certainly give it to you. Your joy will be a river overflowing its banks!*

John 16:21-24

What are we supposed to do when we are facing the everyday trials of life?

What does He say He will do?

Key thought for today:

Straight Talk?

I will say it straight. I don't think any woman forgets the pain of childbirth, especially a c-section. I do not agree with this translation of the original text. I interpret it to say that it overwrites the pain or makes it not the center focus anymore. There isn't much more special or closer to God's gift of life than giving birth. When one decides the risk of their own life for another life to be born is worth it and delivers life despite the pain, stitches, surgery and permanent damage to their body, it is a miracle. Jesus compares His return to this miracle because He calls the trials we endure now as birth pangs. I remember the Braxton-Hicks pre-birth false labor pains that scared me so much with my oldest son. They caused a lot of worry because I had already lost a child to miscarriage so the pains of labor made me rush to the hospital. They assessed me and told me these were normal and just helping my body be ready for the real thing. Many of our trials we are going through are just this. They are moments of stress upon our lives that bring us back to the place where we must live in order to fully be ready for the times ahead. Meanwhile, what are we to do? We are to ask the Father for what we need in Jesus' name and according to His will and in keeping with what He has shown us, then He will most certainly give it to us so that our joy will be like a river overflowing the banks. Just remember rivers overflow because the storm of rain comes first just like labor before the joy of birth. If you are in a trial, ask God for what you need, it is in keeping with His favor for you.

Jesus said these things. Then, raising his eyes in prayer, he said: Father, it's time. Display the bright splendor of your Son
So the Son in turn may show your bright splendor. You put him in charge of everything human
So he might give real and eternal life to all in his care. And this is the real and eternal life: That they know you,
The one and only true God, And Jesus Christ, whom you sent. I glorified you on earth By completing down to the last detail
What you assigned me to do. And now, Father, glorify me with your very own splendor, The very splendor I had in your presence
Before there was a world. - John 17:1-5

In this scripture, what is Jesus asking the Father?

How easy it is to slide into doubt that He knows us, but how easy it is if we choose to trust. How do we develop this trust?

Key thought for today:

Down to the Last Detail?

As I prepared for the party, I discovered that the details mattered. Not just the overview, not just the beginning, not the ending and the after alone, but the details matter! Understanding the last details matters. Jesus said these things. He prayed for the Father to display the bright splendor of the Son so His splendor could show to all. Jesus was put in charge of everything human down to the last details of the real and eternal life. Jesus completed each and every thing to the last details so that we could have the real and eternal life. The very splendor that He had in God's presence before there was a world is the splendor that our glorious eternal existence is made up of in Heaven. If Jesus says He is in charge of the details then we can trust that every little thing to the tiniest minutiae will be thought of, planned for and worked out for our favor. How easy it is to slide into doubt that He knows us, but how easy it is if we choose to trust. Trust doesn't just happen. It is developed in relationship and through prayer/conversation as well as time spent. If we do not take the time to invest in Him and in our relationship with Him, then we allow doubt to get a toehold which soon becomes more when we begin to look around us at others. As I prepare for this party, I love one of the sayings from this artist that has taken root in my soul as it aligns with what Jesus is saying to us, "there are no mistakes, just happy little accidents that are on their way into a masterpiece". We are destined for great things. We need to trust that He has us in His hand!!

Father, I want those you gave me To be with me, right where I am, So they can see my glory, the splendor you gave me, Having loved me Long before there ever was a world. Righteous Father, the world has never known you, But I have known you, and these disciples know That you sent me on this mission. I have made your very being known to them— Who you are and what you do— And continue to make it known, So that your love for me Might be in them Exactly as I am in them. - John 17:24-26

Can you imagine a God, a King who would leave all He had for your sake, to come and dwell among man, then after all the complete hate and disregard, would still plead to His Father in Glory on your behalf to have life in His splendor just for you believing He is who He says He is?

He wants you to be with Him, right where He is. Do you know Him?

Key thought for today:

Do You Know Him?

In John 17, Jesus' final Earthly intercession for us is recorded. Jesus beseeches God the Father on our behalf to be able to come to know Him in all His splendor. The splendor of a king clothed in majesty makes all the world stand up and take notice of all the pomp and circumstance of their station. Can you imagine the King of Kings-The Creator of the World passing by? Moses saw only a glimpse of His train filling His temple and he glowed so much that the people had to put a veil over him to look at him. No man has seen, no eye, no ear has heard the wonders prepared for us but Jesus promised this place and He prayed His final prayer that we as His be with Him. God's love as the Righteous Father will dole out punishment to all who reject His son because His sacrifice is remembered for all time. I love this picture because it looks like hands holding the sun but gives the understanding that the whole world is in His hands. Do you know this king who came to Earth as a babe, grew and suffered all that man could throw at Him even to death on a cross then chose to pray/intercede for you to be with Him in His kingdom in all the splendor and glory? Do you know this righteous Father who gave His son for your sins and prepared this future for you? Can you imagine a God, a King who would leave all He had for your sake, to come and dwell among man, then after all the complete hate and disregard, would still plead to His Father in Glory on your behalf to have life in His splendor just for you believing He is who He says He is? Take time to read His final prayer for you. He wants you to be with Him, right where He is. Do you know Him? If not, May I introduce you to this friend of mine, this King of Glory?

Seek God while he's here to be found, pray to him while he's close at hand.
Let the wicked abandon their way of life and the evil their way of thinking.
Let them come back to God, who is merciful,
come back to our God, who is lavish with forgiveness. - Isaiah 55:6-7

What would you do if you knew today was your very last day on Earth?

If you knew that you would draw your last breath, say your last word, reach out to the last person, and do your last deed today, what would you say, do or be?

Key thought for today:

Close At Hand?

Close at hand is a phrase used to mean easily accessible or easily located. When someone or something is close at hand, they are within the current vicinity or near. As my son prepares to leave, I hug him as he is close at hand for me to express my love. I attended a funeral yesterday where a lady told me how saddened she was that she had not been able to say a proper goodbye in the moment to the one who passed over because she waited too long and the moment slipped away without her knowing it. Too often we are too busy or absorbed in our own things when we have those we love present with us. So many times I hear the "if only we had" or "I wish I had known, then I would have". Today is a fragile piece of time that passes too quickly and it is fleeting. If only, I wish, and so many more expressions of regret do not change the circumstances. We only have the amount of time we are allotted and then judgment. Isaiah as a prophet knew this as he advised us thousands of years ago to "seek God while He's here to be found and pray to Him while He is close at hand" because the hour is darkening and time is swiftly changing to the hour of judgment. He says "let them come back to God, who is merciful, come back to God who is lavish with forgiveness" because God is nearer than He has ever been to us waiting for us to step back into His presence and away from all the distractions that have stolen our attention. He is eager to see us abandon our wicked way of life and the evil ways of thinking and draw near to Him. Seeking God means to spend time searching His word, praying in relationship to Him and trusting Him to be all He says that He is. Coming back to God means realizing that we left and making that turn towards His ways again. Some people are told that their time is short and they need to prepare because of illness but the truth is that the time is short for all of us. What would you do if you knew today was your very last day on Earth? If you knew that you would draw your last breath, say your last word, reach out to the last person, and do your last deed today, what would you say, do or be? Every moment could be our very last. Every moment could be that moment where things change forever. Seek God while He's here to be found and pray to Him while He is close at hand for today could be your last moment for repentance and truth, forgiveness and trust. Tomorrow isn't promised. Today is the last of that moment of today that you will experience. Time is the only thing you can never get back. Live every moment as if it was your last and seek God while He's closer than the breath you breathe.

For the Lord God is a sun and shield; The Lord will give grace and glory;
No good thing will He withhold From those who walk uprightly.
O Lord of hosts, Blessed is the man who trusts in You! - Psalms 84:11-12

What does it mean; God is a sun and shield?

No good thing will He withhold from those who walk uprightly; Does this mean we can have everything we want?

Key thought for today:

Good Things?

Psalms 33:18 states this same concept but I love the simplicity of this restatement in Psalms 84:11. In fact, it is one of my favorite verses of all time because it is a promise of good things. This time of year as the beautiful moon reflects out over the water, it reminds me of this verse so often. It says God is a sun meaning He lights up our world and shields us from evil. His word says, The Lord will give grace and glory. He will be gracious to us who do not deserve it and He will lift us up. Then it has a related clause. This is important because it states the promise that No good thing will He withhold from those who walk uprightly, head high in who God is. This is clear but oh how we often miss it. We believe that because we want it, it is a good thing but the truth is that there are many things we perceive as good that actually maim and kill our souls, our brains and our spirit as well as harming our flesh. I love that this passage closes with Blessed is the person who trusts in God because that is the fulfillment of the promise. Things may not look good but God is good and He has us in His hand so if we trust His ways, we are blessed and we will have all that is good for us. No good thing will be withheld from us as we walk uprightly in Him, not with our head down, not beat down, crawling around, stomping and whining but uprightly. Walking in His grace and goodness, confident that He has what is best in store for us is the way He wants us to live. He wants us to walk according to His plan trusting that He has all things working together for our good, no matter what it looks like. As I look at the moon, I realize that all it does is reflect the light of the sun but it gets a lot of glory. It doesn't even have its own light. It just reflects the sun. What if we were set as confident in the world as the moon? Just reflecting The Son all day long, confident that it is enough to just be His reflecting place, that is what I want to be....then the promise is attained.

"So you'll go out in joy, you'll be led into a whole and complete life.
The mountains and hills will lead the parade, bursting with song.
All the trees of the forest will join the procession, exuberant with applause.
No more thistles, but giant sequoias, no more thornbushes, but stately pines-
Monuments to me, to God, living and lasting evidence of God." - Isaiah 55:12-13

When was the last time you gave God exuberant applause?

How do hills sing and trees clap?

How does loud, exuberant praise change your perspective?

Key thought for today:

Exuberant Applause?

When was the last time you gave God exuberant applause? I know you have clapped excitedly for your kids or grandkids, employees or employers, people receiving awards, singers, songwriters, movie-stars, sports awards or even just a good play lately. But when is the last time you exuberantly praised God with complete and whole joy? The song says, "The hills are alive with the sound of music" ...and they are. God says they will lead the parade bursting with song and the trees will join exuberantly with applause. How do hills sing and trees clap? They grow, they are the reflection of God's glory; the wind of God's breath makes the whistling sound and the clapping of the branches. Giant sequoias and stately pines emerge undeterred by time to worship God in majestic awe and you will do the same when you see them. Monuments to God they are, these mountains and trees. Monuments to man are being torn down and replaced daily but God has monuments that no man can touch. He writes His images through the aurora lights daily and paints the sky and so much more. When is the last time you truly praised God loudly and exuberantly with your whole being? It changes things. It is powerful. It brings the joy of a whole and complete life. I challenge you today! Go out and scream, "Go get 'em God". Go Say Thank you Jesus at the top of your lungs. Go worship, clap, holler and praise...then watch what doors open at the powerhouse of praise!

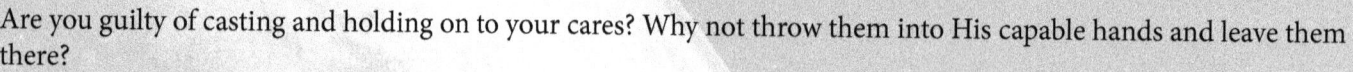

Cast your burden on the Lord, And He shall sustain you;
He shall never permit the righteous to be moved. - Psalms 55:22

Are you guilty of casting and holding on to your cares? Why not throw them into His capable hands and leave them there?

Is it time to make that list and throw it away? You can do this today, either symbolically or even physically. It's time to walk in the freedom He has for you.

Key thought for today:

Casting?

"Pile your troubles on God's shoulders— he'll carry your load, he'll help you out.
He'll never let good people topple into ruin.
Psalms 55:22 MSG
There are many versions of scripture and I usually read them all and tend to use an easier translation when typing my devotionals but this morning God awoke me with this song on my heart.
"I Cast All My Cares Upon You"

My heart has been heavy for several situations that I cannot do anything about except watch them play out. These have weighed me down so much because I have been carrying them in prayer and dwelling on what I could do until He clearly spoke this to my heart. You see casting isn't handing it to someone nor putting it to the side for a bit so you can pick it back up. When you cast, you throw something forcefully and purposefully. If you cast it to God, you are throwing it to Him to take it to do what He will. When God catches our cares, they become fully His to remold and remake. When a potter casts a piece of sculpture or vessel, it is formed carefully and then fired to become a masterpiece. Take your care and cast it to Him like a chunk of clay so He can cast it into the perfect shape that He desires then fire it into a masterpiece of beauty for His glory. It doesn't matter how large or small the situation is, He cares for you. He cares for the person or circumstances you are casting to Him. Today I had to physically write down my concerns on paper then I literally chunked them to God. I needed to physically release them from burdening me. I needed to feel the physical release of tossing them like rocks away from me into a place I could not go get them again. I do not know your circumstances but if you are like me and you tend to carry a load that you were never meant to carry, it might be high time for you to get some physical action into tossing and casting your situation into prayers and stop drawing them back on the fishing line. See that is my tendency, too. I cast them with a line attached and slowly reel them back into me where they have then gathered more problems and issues and become super weighty. This isn't what God wants. Cut the line. Toss the ball to Him. Let Him carry it. He has a more than capable ability to manage it. Give it to Him and trust that He will work it all out for your good. Casting. Such a release. I want to be cast into the role God has for me and not carry these burdens anymore. Cast your thoughts. Cast your cares. Cast your vote for God. Cast and walk away into the freedom role He has for you built by trusting Him.

Each one of these people of faith died not yet having in hand what was promised, but still believing.
How did they do it? They saw it way off in the distance, waved their greeting, and accepted the fact that they were transients in this world.
People who live this way make it plain that they are looking for their true home. If they were homesick for the old country, they could have
gone back any time they wanted. But they were after a far better country than that—heaven country.
You can see why God is so proud of them, and has a City waiting for them. - Hebrews 11:13-16

How did those who lived and walked with God have the faith to continue on?

What then is your motivation to carry His message

Key thought for today:

In Hand?

Hebrews 11 is considered the faith chapter. It talks about the acts of faith that were performed by those who lived and walked with God before the new covenant. In verse 13 it is summed up that each of them were people of faith, and yet they died, not having in hand what was promised. It gives the example of the faith they walked in and the promises received from that faith but then says they died not yet having in hand what was promised. Then it asks, How did they do it? They saw it afar off in the distance. Some things we are promised, we will never see until we are in the Promised Land of Heaven. But we have "in hand" examples of the walk, a map, a path walked before us. Abram was promised that his seed would number more than the sands and they have and do but he is receiving greater still even now. Moses was promised a land flowing with milk and honey for his people where they now live but he is receiving his milk and honey in Heaven as he never walked into that land on Earth. God is proud of those who are faithful despite the trials and has a home waiting to receive us that is beyond our wildest imagination but we must first get our eyes off the things of Earth. We must begin to view our world through other eyes-those with Heavenly purpose. This world is about to be shaken to its core in every way. All that is known and beloved will be shaken because God must get our vision off the temporal. The old saying goes "a bird in hand is worth two in the bush" meaning work with what you have but in Heavenly vision, those two in the bush are being productive for future generations. The things of Earth may look bleak some days. You might feel worn down and worn out but your purpose is to point all you meet to He who is. If you are pointing, sharing and telling in your everyday walk, that is all you can do. I saw a family standing on the side of the road struggling to make ends meet with a baby. I stopped and brought them food of Earth, for the now, but I stopped to tell them of Heaven. I told them of God's goodness and His promises. I told them that He will not leave them nor forsake them. They were Muslim and had not heard of God in this manner. I gave them a Bible, shared the moment and ministered with the few minutes I had off for lunch. I planted a seed that God will use. This is my purpose. Whether you plant, water, till the ground, fertilize or harvest, it is your role to look towards the future of His promise. We have "in hand" the ability to confirm our faith. We have "in hand" examples of promises delivered and promises fulfilled. We have "in hand" so much, but we must be faithful to look ahead and reach out to those who do not have it "in hand" and we must cling to the faith we are taught until that time of our reward. We are after a far better country than the one we live in. We are after Heaven.

"If only my words were written in a book— better yet, chiseled in stone!
Still, I know that God lives—the One who gives me back my life— and eventually he'll take his stand on earth.
And I'll see him—even though I get skinned alive!— see God myself, with my very own eyes.
Oh, how I long for that day! - Job 19:23-27

What type of suffering are you enduring for Christ?

What will you choose to do about it?

Key thought for today:

Skinned Alive?

I fell yesterday and skinned my whole left side of my body and both hands on the concrete as I skidded across it. My body is feeling beaten and bruised. My spirit has felt that way for a while as so much has come against me that I feel raw. This is how Job felt as he penned these words. He was journaling his thoughts as he suffered through, completely not understanding why he was walking through the trials. He deeply wished for a book to read his words of praise to God. He desperately wanted to see God and was holding onto the promise of His return with all he had. Job suffered as no man on Earth has suffered in the flesh except Christ. He suffered so much in his trials because he was faithful. Yes, I said that right. Because he was faithful, he suffered for God. What type of suffering are you enduring for Christ? Many of us go through heavy trials of financial burdens, physical ailments or emotional trauma but we see these as life events and experiences rather than the suffering of the cross. We fail to recognize the glory of the cross in our sacrifices. I am thinking of so many of my sweet friends who suffer through dementia, cancer, financial loss, disappointment, dashed dreams and more. All of this suffering is not about Earth. It is about His glory. I will glory in the cross so His suffering will not be in vain. I will not cling to the cross as a place of suffering but a place of glory. I will not allow my sorrows and let downs to be a place of suffering anymore. I will choose instead for them to be places of praise. You see it is in our mindset. I can understand that I fell and moan about the pain or I can glory that when I fell, I didn't break a leg or hip or my back. I can choose the sorrow or the glory. I choose His story! I choose His glory. Still, I Know that God lives-the One who gives me back my life daily and eventually He will take His stand on Earth. Job didn't see the days Christ walked the Earth and he didn't see the cross nor was there a book with a record of it all. We have so much to be grateful for in our lives. We can choose a lifestyle of bemoaning what we don't have or we can choose a lifetime of praise through the storms. I choose praise. I look at this beautiful photo of the Northern lights looking like the bottom of a bridal skirt twirling in dance and I think of the days and nights of dancing in praise that we will do in Heaven. I wonder which skirt tail from one of my sweet friends in Heaven this was? There is coming a day. Oh, how I long for that day! Until that day, though I be skinned alive, I will choose praise through the big and the small trials and through the massive storms! My words can be written in a book and they can be chiseled on stone but lest these words be words of praise, the rocks themselves will cry out. Let my words be words of praise for all He is, no matter what!

"Here's another way to put it: You're here to be light, bringing out the God-colors in the world. God is not a secret to be kept. We're going public with this, as public as a city on a hill. If I make you light-bearers, you don't think I'm going to hide you under a bucket, do you? I'm putting you on a light stand. Now that I've put you there on a hilltop, on a light stand—shine! Keep open house; be generous with your lives. By opening up to others, you'll prompt people to open up with God, this generous Father in heaven. - Matthew 5:14-16

Wondering why God isn't doing wonders in your life? Are you hiding your light?

Who is looking at you? Are they seeing sparkles or storm clouds? What draws them to God if you are their light?

Key thought for today:

Open House?

My neighbor's house just sold after several open house events. It is a beautiful home situated on 2 acres and has lots to recommend it but without seeing it, pictures are just not enough. At the open house, people could experience the home and picture themselves living there in their minds. God wants us to be open houses so that people can see His love through us. He said He wants us to be generous with our lives so that by our openness, we will prompt others to open up to God, our Father in Heaven. He wants us to be light, attract others to Him by our acknowledgment of who He is. A lot of people ask me why I am so open about things in my life. This is why. God wants us to be light bearers to demonstrate to others that He is not a secret to be kept but a revelation to all. He brings out God-colors in this world. One day I will go see the Northern Lights in person but until then, I picture these God-colors of the world as what we should be to those around us. We should be the dancing lights in the darkness of life. We should shine and sparkle through our darkest nights and the storms of life so others may know that God. Life isn't always like we dream it will be. There are lots of storms and trials but we still have the choice to sparkle in the darkness as God's light. He has called us to be light bearers, cities on hills and lamps on a lamp stand without a shade. He has called us to stand forth publicly bearing His name. Wondering why God isn't doing wonders in your life? Remove the lampshade. Let others see your light. Begin to sparkle in His praise. It is said that a star is millions of miles away yet we see its sparkle. Who is looking at you? Are they seeing sparkles or storm clouds? What draws them to God if you are their light? Time to remove that which is hiding our lights and allow His praise to sparkle through us despite the storms. Through it all, that is how they know God is real. Go Sparkle!

Use your heads as you live and work among outsiders. Don't miss a trick. Make the most of every opportunity. Be gracious in your speech. The goal is to bring out the best in others in a conversation, not put them down, not cut them out. - Colossians 4:5-6

The Goal is to achieve what matters most. So what matters most?

What is your life speaking? Are you speaking the name of Jesus to the hurting? To bring healing?

Are you reaching that one in gracious conversation or are you too busy arguing your position or opinion?

Are you bringing out the best in others or are you too busy watching out for yourself to be the love He called you to be?

Key thought for today:

What Matters Most?

The Goal is to achieve what matters most. So what matters most? In Colossians, we are instructed that the goal is to bring out the best in others in a conversation, not cut them out and not put others down. We are instructed to be gracious in our speech and make the most of every opportunity as we live and work among those who do not know Jesus. Use our heads and not miss a trick but make the most sounds like the way to get ahead of others but instead it is a way to empower others and embrace our purpose. Paul is instructing and referring others as he requests prayer that every time he opens his mouth, those around him hear Jesus. What a worthy goal! What a precious standard of what matters most! Our lives have a purpose, to shine the light of His love through our words, deeds and conversations. What matters most is that we draw others to Him in our ways and this is the how. Be gracious. I love the song, "I Speak The Name of Jesus Over You", because it is exactly what we should do in our everyday lives. What matters most in life isn't how much money we make or what we own or who we know, as all this fades moments after we step into eternity. What matters most is that we make the most of every opportunity to speak Jesus to others not as a put down or a cut down to their lifestyle but in truth and love. What is your life speaking? Are you speaking the name of Jesus to the hurting? To bring healing? Are you reaching that one in gracious conversation or are you too busy arguing your position or opinion? Are you bringing out the best in others or are you too busy watching out for yourself to be the love He called you to be? Use your head and His heart. Be His hand extended in graciousness to those around you. Speak the name of Jesus through your words, your deeds and your conversations because that is the goal-what matters most is Him.

Jesus answered them, "Do you finally believe? In fact, you're about to make a run for it—
saving your own skins and abandoning me. But I'm not abandoned. The Father is with me.
I've told you all this so that trusting me, you will be unshakable and assured, deeply at peace.
In this godless world you will continue to experience difficulties. But take heart! I've conquered the world."
John 16:31-33

What are you running to?

Are you lost in His love, clinging to His promise, wrapped in His praise?

So Jesus asks: Do you finally believe?

Key thought for today:

Difficulties?

I love the way Jesus just shoots straight with His words. He knew exactly how the disciples would act and how we act when things get tough. We make a run for it, trying to save ourselves and abandon others. It is human nature but not God's nature. Finding our way back to our natural selves in God is finding the place of assurance. One of my favorite songs of all time is "Blessed Assurance". Fanny Crosby spent her life blind in Earthly vision but wrote over 8000 songs of worship plus much more. She found that her assurances weren't in men and their ways. So Jesus asks: Do you finally believe? Trusting in Him leaves you deeply at peace, unshakable and assured when it looks like all will fall. This is a Godless world but filled with many idols that people have made into God in their lives from movie stars to iPhones and social media. We must prioritize Jesus and realize that He is our peace. We must take heart when the world quakes. We must realize that difficulties exist and will still come but we must rest in the knowledge of His blessed assurance in our lives when the world is quaking. Jesus says He shares all this so that trusting in Him will make us confident And assured!

What are you running to? Be still and know that He is God! Are you lost in His love, clinging to His promise, wrapped in His praise? This is the place of Blessed Assurance.

My dear, dear friends, if God loved us like this, we certainly ought to love each other.
No one has seen God, ever. But if we love one another,
God dwells deeply within us, and his love becomes complete in us—perfect love!
1 John 4:11-12

Know someone hard to love? See God instead of them.

Will you allow God to be seen through His love in you despite the circumstances?

Key thought for today:

Seen God Lately?

I guess by now it must be obvious that I am fascinated with the aurora lights since it is the background to most of my pictures throughout this whole devotional series. Why they fascinate me is that they are a very evident example of a God who sees us and knows us. I know the scientists will say they are just geomagnetic storms like lightning but, I know they are more. Although I have yet to see them in person, I have seen evidence of them in photos and videos which are just incredible. In 1st John, the author tells us that no one has seen God but His love in our lives is evidence of Him. God dwells deeply within all of us and when His love becomes perfected in us, the evidence is all over us so that we love deeply, wholly and fully. I tell people often that I love them because I truly do. I do not intimately know everyone I love but I love them because they are a part of who I am just as one particle of light makes up this beautiful light show called the northern lights. Each particle of energy is important to the beauty of this show just as each person is important to the evidence of God's love. Yes, there are people who are harder to love than others. They are not impossible to love as God loves them. It takes all kinds of lights and energy to spark and make this terrific light show just like it takes all kinds of people and personalities to truly light our world with God's love. His love is deep and wide, strong and true. His love isn't limited by me or you. His love is perfected when we love those that are hard to love. When we love in His love instead of our own love, we sparkle differently than just a reflection like the moon and stars. We sparkle in a tangible and felt way so that the love is felt when we walk in a room. We carry a difference in us that makes the energy in a room feel differently charged. It is love charged, love perfected, love enduring and love complete. Because God loved us so completely, deeply, and perfectly that He was willing to sacrifice His own son to bridge the gap created by our willfulness, then our love through Him is made complete by accepting His sacrifice for us. When a bridge connects, it doesn't become unconnected. It may get blocked or not have good flow or functionality because we clutter it with other stuff but once we plug into the love of God, we love. The wholeness of His love cannot be taken away if lessened or marred. It is His perfect love. The way we demonstrate it is by loving others including those who are a little prickly and hard to embrace. Love isn't less. Love doesn't shrink. Love doesn't die or go away. This is why death, divorce and separation are so hard. Our love is an energy that sparks in our lives and the magnetic magnificence of His love in us is like these auroras. Sometimes these lights are loudly on display in perfect beautiful splendor and other times they are quieter and not seen as evidently. The love like the lights is always there. There may be clouds that cover it up or storms that disturb it, but know that the storms make the love stronger and richer. I hate divorce, death, separation and pain. I know these are disruptions to God's love but they do not stop it, change it nor make it disappear. In fact, these hard situations make His love more evident because just like lightning and lights sparkle more in disruptions, His love is more tangible in us in hard times when we push into Him. I don't know your situation nor your disruptions in your life, but I do know His love is made perfect when we are not strong. He carries us when we cannot carry on. We are raised up in His power in our weakness because His strength is perfect. His love, not ours. His power and strength not ours. Know someone hard to love? See God instead of them. Let His love be made perfect in you by loving the unlovable. Remember it takes a refraction of light through to see a rainbow of promise. The light and love are always there, you just cannot see them without the storms that cause the refraction. Embrace the bad through Him. Allow God to be seen through His love in you despite the circumstances.

God means what he says. What he says goes. His powerful Word is sharp as a surgeon's scalpel, cutting through everything, whether doubt or defense, laying us open to listen and obey. Nothing and no one can resist God's Word. We can't get away from it—no matter what.
Hebrews 4:12-13

Are you struggling? Time for some Word Surgery.

You don't understand The Why? Word Surgery.

You feel overwhelmed and tired. Word Surgery

Key thought for today:

Word Surgery?

As I close out this thirteenth set of devotionals, the truth of God's word stands alone as a powerful tool. God's word isn't ever void. He means what He says and all nature bows to His commands. His word isn't a clumsy tool but a surgical scalpel that cuts clean, sharp and smooth. My niece recently had surgery and I know exactly how she feels right after surgery as I have been under that scalpel over 20 times in the last few years. That raw feeling of openness lays each part of you available to the Surgeon. My pastor often says that when He is preaching, it gets quiet like a room in surgery as God speaks. The truth is that His word cuts and heals simultaneously. I think of this photo with the Northern Lights and The Milky Way in the same photo side by side. God created the universe, directs the actions and speaks peace all at once. He is able to use a storm to clear a path and make the way or He can send a quiet wind or word. He is The Great Physician and the Healer. He is both the Provider and the Judge. He is The Source and The Living Water. He is The Lion of Judah and The Lamb of God. He is Alpha and Omega, Beginning and Ending, Truth and Justice, Present and Eternal. He is The Light that speaks out the light to the darkness. He is The Seed, The Water, The Sower and The Harvester. He Is. God means what He says, says what He means and what He says IS! Nothing and no one can resist God's word. We cannot escape it no matter how some of us try. Whatever your circumstances, you can trust this. His word is forever because He is The Word. The Big Bang Theory and Evolution are just mythological premises in His world. He is, was and always will be. Are you struggling? Time for some Word Surgery. Get His word out and begin to speak its truths as it will not return void. You don't understand The Why? Word Surgery. Begin to quote His promises. You feel overwhelmed and tired. Word Surgery-His word is Life, Living Water...find your promise and your potential and your hopes and your dreams and your healing and your future all in Him. It is all in His word. His Word gives us Spirit Wings. We can rise above it to conquer it all in His truth-so start the Word Surgery. Cut out the cancers that suck your life through His word surgery and move into His promises.